Cambridge English

OFFICIAL
PREPARATION MATERIAL

Garan Holcombe
Series Editor: Annette Capel

Prepare!

WORKBOOK

Level 3

Cambridge University Press
www.cambridge.org/elt

Cambridge English Language Assessment
www.cambridgeenglish.org

Information on this title: www.cambridge.org/9780521180559

© Cambridge University Press and UCLES 2015

First published 2015
20 19 18 17 16 15 14 13 12 11 10 9 8 7

Printed in Spain by GraphyCems

A catalogue record for this publication is available from the British Library

ISBN 978-0-521-18054 -2 Student's Book
ISBN 978-1-107-49740-5 Student's Book and Online Workbook
ISBN 978-1-107-49735-1 Student's Book and Online Workbook with Testbank
ISBN 978-0-521-18055-9 Workbook with Audio
ISBN 978-0-521-18056-6 Teacher's Book with DVD and Teacher's Resources Online
ISBN 978-0-521-18057-3 Class Audio CDs
ISBN 978-1-107-49732-0 Presentation Plus DVD-ROM

Downloadable audio for this publication at www.cambridge.org/PrepareAudio

Contents

VOCABULARY

1 Put the letters in the right order to make adjectives.

0	n i d k	k ..ind..........
1	z a y l	l ....
2	l o p e i t	p ....
3	r e d i n l f y	f ....
4	n f y u n	f ....
5	y u b s	b ....
6	s a l p e d e	p ....
7	l o u p r a p	p ....

2 Complete the sentences with adjectives from Exercise 1.

0 Dad is ...kind.... to us. He always helps my brothers and me with our homework.

1 My brother's very .... at work at the moment. He starts at 6.30 every morning!

2 Fernanda is so .... ! She just sits on the sofa all day.

3 Tanya is the most .... girl in school. Everyone likes her.

4 My cousin is very .... He makes everyone laugh.

5 My parents were really .... when I did well in my English exam.

GRAMMAR   Present simple and present continuous

3 Choose the right words to complete the email.

Hi Sergei

I'm camping in Ireland! Every day we **(0)** *get* / *are getting* up early and **(1)** *cook* / *are cooking* breakfast. Then we wash up and have a shower.

It's beautiful here. I **(2)** *have* / *'m having* a great time and learning lots of new things. The weather **(3)** *changes* / *is changing* so quickly, but I like that.

Everyone **(4)** *does* / *is doing* different sports at the moment. But I'm feeling tired, so I **(5)** *write* / *'m writing* to you on an old computer.

Love

Monica

4 Complete the sentences with the present simple or present continuous form of the verbs.

0 He usually ...reads... stories about detectives. He ...'s reading... one about a football player tonight. (read)

1 My sister usually .... tennis at school. She .... in the park today. (play)

2 Mum usually .... to music on the radio. Today she .... to it on her MP3 player. (listen)

3 My brother usually .... his homework in his room. He .... it in the library today. (do)

4 My sister usually .... a violin lesson on Mondays. Today she .... a piano lesson. (have)

5 Complete the sentences with the present simple or present continuous form of the verbs in the box.

~~go~~   learn   make   play   teach   watch

0 My sister ....*goes*.... swimming every evening after school.

1 I .... a film on TV now, so I can't come to the café.

2 My aunt .... biology in a university.

3 We .... basketball on Mondays and volleyball on Wednesdays.

4 My parents usually .... pizzas for everyone on Friday nights.

5 My friend .... Chinese at the moment.

6 Write complete sentences.

0 I / do / my homework / at the moment
...*I'm doing my homework at the moment.*...

1 They / play football / in the park / now
....

2 My brother / go to the cinema / on / Friday evenings
....
....

3 He / visit his cousins / on / Sunday afternoons
....

4 My parents / shop / in the supermarket / at the moment
....
....

5 We / meet in the café / every Saturday
....

6 She / usually / see her friends / at the weekend
....

7 Choose the right words to complete the sentences.

1 What *do you usually do* / *are you usually doing* at the weekends?

2 My mum *is teaching* / *teaches* me how to make bread at the moment.

3 We *don't go* / *aren't going* to the park after school on Wednesdays.

4 *Are you having* / *Do you have* your dinner now?

5 My parents *don't play* / *aren't playing* golf on Saturdays.

8 ☉ Students often make mistakes with the present simple and the present continuous. Correct the mistakes in these sentences.

0 She is going to work every day, but at the weekend she is free.
...*She goes to work every day, but at*...
...*the weekend she is free.*...

1 Every day in the morning we are eating soup.
....
....

2 She study medicine at Odessa University.
....

3 Anna goes to college every day. She learns English.
....
....

4 When you are coming, bring your best clothes.
....

5 I write this email because I want to tell you about my last trip.
....
....

LISTENING

9 ▶2 Listen to Mr Smith talking to his class about a camping trip. Complete the sentences with numbers.

1 Mr Smith is telling Class .... B about this year's camping trip.

2 The trip costs £..................... .

3 The trip is for .... nights.

4 .... students can go on the trip.

5 If students want to go, they must give their forms to Mr Smith by .... am on Monday.

10 ▶2 Listen again and choose the right answer (a or b).

0 The camping trip is to ....
  ⓐ France   **b** Spain

1 Students .... play volleyball at the campsite.
  a can   **b** can't

2 Students can't play .... at the campsite.
  a tennis   **b** video games

3 Students can win awards for ....
  a swimming and football
  b climbing and hiking

4 Parents must write Mr Smith ....
  a a letter   **b** an email

Fill in the form with your details

VOCABULARY

1 **Match the numbers to the words.**

1	0441	**a**	oh double one four
2	770630	**b**	double oh seven oh three six
3	007036	**c**	double seven oh six three oh
4	0114	**d**	oh double four one

2 **Write the email addresses.**

0 p dot sanchez at life dot com
....p.sanchez@life.com....................................

1 burak dot guner at web dot com

....

2 me at internet dot co dot uk

....

3 klara dot bort at poland dot net

....

3 **Complete the sentences with the names in the box.**

> Batman   Sherlock Holmes   Superman and Lois Lane

1 .... lives at 221B Baker Street, London, UK.

2 .... live at 1938 Sullivan Lane, Metropolis, USA.

3 .... lives at Wayne Manor, Gotham City, USA.

READING

4 Choose the right words (a or b) to complete the blog.

Margarita's daily story

Today I'm **(0)** ...b.... about my sister, Leticia. It's her sixteenth birthday tomorrow. She is two years older than me.
Leticia is very **(1)** .... She always helps me with my maths homework – she loves numbers, but I hate them. She's teaching me tango at the moment. I'm very **(2)** .... about it. Tango is difficult, but Leticia is good at dancing and she's a good teacher too. We have **(3)** .... together. My sister is interested in everything! She **(4)** .... books about science, she does lots of sports, she likes camping, and she's **(5)** .... to play the piano. She can't play very well yet, but she practises every day. She'd also like to learn the violin. Leticia is **(6)** .... too. She always makes me laugh.

	a		b
0	write	**b**	writing
1	**a** busy	**b**	kind
2	**a** pleased	**b**	polite
3	**a** funny	**b**	fun
4	**a** reads	**b**	reading
5	**a** learn	**b**	learning
6	**a** funny	**b**	lazy

5 Read the blog again. Are the sentences right (✔) or wrong (✗)?

0 Margarita is seventeen. .....✗....
1 Leticia doesn't like numbers. ....
2 Margarita doesn't think tango is easy. ....
3 Margarita likes learning tango. ....
4 Leticia isn't interested in many things. ....
5 Leticia doesn't play the violin. ....

WRITING

6 Complete the texts with the correct form of the verbs in the boxes.

do   do   sleep

Marek is very popular because he's very funny. But he doesn't do anything! He **(1)** .... for fifteen hours a day, he never **(2)** .... his homework, and he sits on the sofa for hours watching TV. He doesn't like **(3)** .... any sports – his only hobby is sleeping.

go   play   study

Alessandro never stops! He **(4)** .... tennis and basketball at the weekend and he **(5)** .... swimming every evening. He really likes learning languages. He's **(6)** .... Russian now.

cook   do   think

Zeynep is the nicest person in the world. She always **(7)** .... of other people's feelings. She likes **(8)** .... meals for her family and she always **(9)** .... the weekly shopping for her grandmother. She even helps me with my homework!

7 Read the descriptions again and answer the questions.

1 Who is very kind? ....
2 Who is very busy? ....
3 Who is very lazy? ....

8 Now write about someone you know. Describe this person and say what they like doing. Use adjectives in your description.

....
....
....
....
....
....

2 The natural world
The world is changing

VOCABULARY

1 Look at the pictures and write the words.

> desert   forest   ~~hill~~   island   lake   mountain   river   sea   valley   volcano

0 .... hill .... 1 .... 2 .... 3 .... 4 ....

5 .... 6 .... 7 .... 8 .... 9 ....

2 Now complete the sentences with words from Exercise 1. Then match the sentences to the pictures.

1 The Nile is a .... in Egypt.
2 Vesuvius is the name of a famous ....
3 Everest is a .... in the Himalayas.
4 Titicaca is a .... between Bolivia and Peru.
5 Cyprus is an .... in the Mediterranean ....
6 The Kalahari is a .... in Botswana, Namibia and South Africa.

a ☐   b ☐   c ☐

d ☐   e ☐   f ☐

GRAMMAR   Verbs we don't usually use in the continuous

3 Look at the verbs we don't usually use in the continuous. Find the odd one out.

0 (run)	believe	know	understand
1 think	own	read	know
2 own	know	do	believe
3 play	write	walk	understand
4 love	like	hate	watch
5 have	own	work	belong to

4 Complete the sentences with the correct form of the verbs in the box.

> believe   belong to   hope   know
> own   understand   want

1 Do you .... Mr Watkins? I think he lives in your street.

2 Sam says his mother is a famous actress, but I don't .... him.

3 I .... the weather is good tomorrow. I really .... to go swimming.

4 My mother .... some Italian, but she doesn't speak it very well.

5 I don't .... a guitar. I use my sister's to practise.

6 That video game .... Kate.

5 Choose the right word to complete the sentences.

1 I *do / 'm doing* my homework now, so I can't come to the park.

2 These books *belong to / are belonging to* Simon.

3 I *like / 'm liking* your hat, Tim. Can I try it on?

4 My dad can't take me to football practice because he *works / 's working* at the moment.

5 Oh, I *hate / 'm hating* this song! Can you turn the radio off, please?

6 *Do you know / Are you knowing* Rachel's brother? He's very funny.

6 ⊙ Students often make mistakes with verbs in the present continuous. Correct the mistakes in three of these sentences. Which two sentences are correct?

1 There is a concert on Saturday. I am hoping you can come.

....

....

2 My parents are making dinner at the moment.

....

3 I think you are liking reading.

....

4 I don't understand this exercise.

....

5 I would like to tell you what I am thinking of Rio de Janeiro.

....

....

READING

7 Complete the email with the words in the box.

> changing   feel   happening   learning
> interesting   reading   understand

Hi Lucia

I'm **(1)** .... a new book at the moment. I don't **(2)** .... everything in the book, but it's very **(3)** .... It's called *This Changing Earth*. It's about what is **(4)** .... to our planet. It's amazing! I am **(5)** .... so much.

We think that we see the same world every day, but we don't. Everything is **(6)** .... all the time.

I **(7)** .... sad, and also angry and excited, when I read the book. I think about everything too. Would you like to read it when I finish it?

Love

Violetta

8 Read the email again and answer the questions.

1 What is Violetta's book called?

....

2 What is the book about?

....

3 Does Violetta like the book?

....

Wild animals

VOCABULARY

1 Find twelve animal words.

d	a	b	p	d	o	g	m
o	b	s	e	v	w	m	o
l	i	o	n	a	e	o	u
p	r	y	g	a	r	n	s
h	d	c	u	r	k	k	e
i	u	a	i	a	z	e	c
n	d	t	n	t	b	y	h
e	l	e	p	h	a	n	t

2 Look at the pictures and write the words from Exercise 1.

1 .... 2 ....

3 .... 4 ....

5 .... 6 .... 7 .... 8 ....

9 .... 10 .... 11 .... 12 ....

3 Read the sentences. Are they right (✔) or wrong (✗)?

1 Monkeys don't eat insects. ....
2 Elephants can live until they are seventy years old. ....
3 There aren't any snakes in Antarctica. ....
4 There aren't any lions living in the wild in Asia. ....
5 Dolphins are very intelligent animals. ....
6 Penguins can fly. ....

LISTENING

EXAM TIPS

Listening Part 2
- Always read the task and questions before you listen.
- You can only use an answer A–H once. Remember you can't use the example!

4 ⬤ ▶3 **Listen to Martha talking to a friend about her trip to the zoo. Which animal was each person most interested in? For questions 1–5, write a letter (A–H) next to each person.**

People		What they liked best
0 brother	E	**A** bears
1 sister	☐	**B** dolphins
2 dad	☐	**C** elephants
3 mum	☐	**D** lions
4 granddad	☐	**E** monkeys
5 grandma	☐	**F** penguins
		G snakes
		H wild dogs

Prepare to write a text about an animal

5 **Choose the right words to complete the text.**

The Black Bear

Black bears live in the forests and mountains of Canada, the USA and Mexico. They usually eat grass and insects, but they eat other things too, **(1)** *including / about* fish, small animals, and the food people leave at campsites. Adult black bears are very big and they weigh **(2)** *between / including* 90 kg and 270 kg.

Scientists think there are **(3)** *around / including* 600,000 of these animals in the wild in North America, but there may be many more. Female black bears have two or three babies in the winter called cubs. They stay with their mother for **(4)** *between / about* two years.

6 **Now write about the African elephant. Use *between*, *around/about*, *including* and this information:**

name:	African elephant
from:	Africa
lives:	forests and grasslands
eats:	leaves, grass, fruit
size:	very big; weighs 2,268 kg – 6,350 kg
age:	lives in wild until around 70
number in the wild:	470,000–690,000
babies:	females have one baby calf every two to four years. Baby elephants weigh about 91 kg when born.

....
....
....
....
....
....
....
....

3 Travel: then and now
She loved adventure

VOCABULARY

1 Complete the travel words.

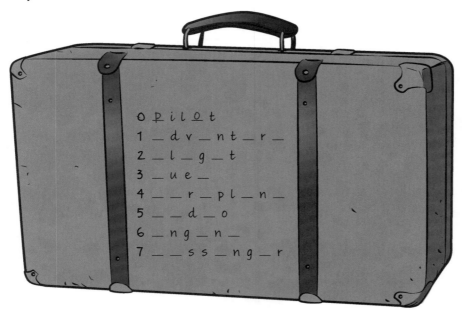

```
0 p i l o t
1 _ d v _ n t _ r _
2 _ l _ g _ t
3 _ u e _
4 _ _ r _ p l _ n _
5 _ _ d _ o
6 _ n g _ n _
7 _ _ s s _ n g _ r
```

2 Now complete the sentences with the words from Exercise 1.

1 We put .... in an engine.
2 An .... is an exciting, unusual or dangerous journey.
3 A pilot uses a .... to talk to people at the airport.
4 A .... travels somewhere by aeroplane, bus or train.
5 A .... flies an aeroplane.
6 *Fly* is the verb. The noun is ....
7 The .... makes the aeroplane move.

GRAMMAR Past simple

3 Match the questions to the answers.

1 What did you think of the film?
2 Which after-school club did you choose?
3 Did Vladimir go to the sports club?
4 How did you get to Moscow?
5 What happened to your arm?
6 Why did Lorena go home?

a She had to go the dentist.
b I broke it playing basketball. It really hurts.
c It was really funny.
d By train. It took a long time!
e History. Did you choose it too?
f No, he went home. He was tired.

4 Which past simple questions need the word *did*?

0 Who ....−......... wanted to climb the old tower?
1 Who .... you see on the plane?
2 Who .... you go on holiday with?
3 Who .... flew the plane?
4 Who .... you meet at the hotel?
5 Who .... found the bags?
6 Who .... spoke to the passengers?

5 Complete the conversation with the past simple form of the verbs in the box.

be	have	go	love
take off	sleep	visit	

Mila: Hi, Seda. How **(1)** .... your trip?

Seda: We **(2)** .... a brilliant time, thanks.

Mila: And the flight? You were worried about that.

Seda: Well, I didn't like it when the plane **(3)** .... You know I don't like flying. But when we flew back at night, I **(4)** .... the whole time!

Mila: What did you do in Rome?

Seda: Everything! We **(5)** .... the Colosseum and the Vatican. We also **(6)** .... to the Forum. I **(7)** .... walking around there.

6 👁 Students often make mistakes with the past simple. Underline the mistakes in these sentences.

1 I went to Mar del Plata. I have a lovely day.
2 Last night I forgot my history book in your house.
3 I went shopping yesterday. I brought a very nice skirt and a sweater.
4 I enjoyed my holiday. The weather was hot. I liked hot weather and I like it when the sun is shining.

7 Now correct the mistakes.

1 ....
....
2 ....
....
3 ....
....
4 ....
....

READING

8 Complete the article with the past simple form of the verbs in the box.

not stop	spend	start
take	travel	wait

Graham's BIG Adventure

It **(1)** .... Graham Hughes four years to visit all 201 countries in the world. And he did it all without taking a flight. He **(2)** .... by boat, bus and train, by taxi and on foot. He **(3)** .... $100 a week on his journey. He **(4)** .... travelling on New Year's Day 2009. Travelling around Europe and South America was easy, but travelling around Asia, Africa and the Caribbean, and getting to small islands in the Pacific and Atlantic, was difficult. He often **(5)** .... for weeks for a boat. But Graham **(6)** .... , and on Monday the 26th of November 2012, the 1426th day of his journey, he arrived in the last country: South Sudan. Graham is the only person to see every country in the world without taking a flight.

9 Read the article again. Are the sentences right (✔) or wrong (✗)?

1 Graham flew around the world. ....
2 He had $400 a month to spend. ....
3 He started travelling on the first of January. ....
4 Travelling around Africa wasn't easy. ....
5 He stopped travelling on the 201st day. ....

How can I help you?

VOCABULARY

1 Put the letters in the right order to make holiday words and phrases.

1 p m a   m........................
2 s t e g u   g........................
3 t r o i s v i   v........................
4 s c u a i s t e   s........................
5 n o l i d y o h a   o........................
6 g e u l g a g   l........................
7 p r t c i e i o s e t n   r........................
8 s u t r o i t   t........................

2 Complete the text with the words from Exercise 1. Use the plural form if necessary.

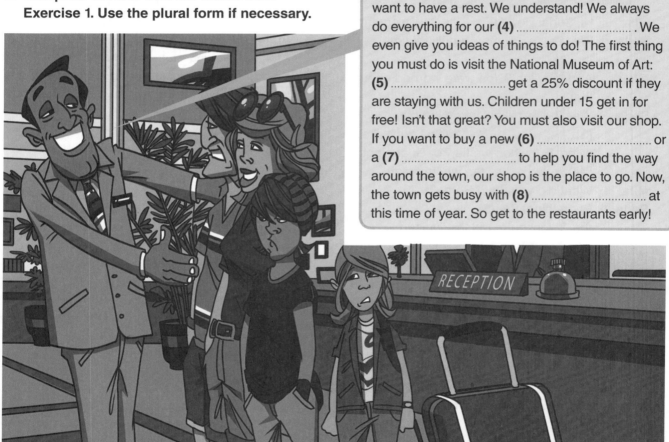

Welcome to the Highland Hotel! Please leave your **(1)** .... at the door. We take that for you. The **(2)** .... has your room key. Now, you are **(3)** .... and want to have a rest. We understand! We always do everything for our **(4)** .... We even give you ideas of things to do! The first thing you must do is visit the National Museum of Art: **(5)** .... get a 25% discount if they are staying with us. Children under 15 get in for free! Isn't that great? You must also visit our shop. If you want to buy a new **(6)** .... or a **(7)** .... to help you find the way around the town, our shop is the place to go. Now, the town gets busy with **(8)** .... at this time of year. So get to the restaurants early!

LISTENING

3 ▶4 Listen to the conversation between Ross and an assistant in the tourist information office. Match the people to the things they like.

1 Ross's mum   **a** football
2 Ross's sister   **b** music
3 Ross   **c** art
4 Ross's dad   **d** old buildings

4 ▶4 Listen again and number the assistant's questions in the right order.

a Do you like music?   ....
b What about football?   ....
c Do you know The Beatles?   ....
d Can I help you?   ....
e Do you like looking at old buildings?   ....
f What about going on the river on a boat?   ....

WRITING

5 Match the descriptions to the places.

VENICE

Venice is a small city in the north of Italy. It's famous around the world for its beautiful old buildings and its bridges. The weather is very good in the spring and summer, but it can be very cold in the winter! If you come in December, bring a hat and scarf! There are lots of places to see in Venice, but these four are very special.

1 You can't come to Venice and not do this! Remember, there aren't any cars here, so people travel around on the water on these beautiful boats called 'gondolas'.

2 Do you love art? Well, this is the place for you. You can spend hours looking at the beautiful old paintings by Renaissance painters such as Veronese, Titian and Tintoretto.

3 This is one of the first places that visitors go to. It's a big open space in the middle of the city. This is the perfect place to walk around and look at the beautiful old buildings.

4 This is one of the oldest things in the city. Walk across it, stand on it, watch the gondolas as they pass underneath. You'll love this!

6 Now write about a city in another country that you are interested in. Include this information:

1 how big the city is
2 what the weather is like
3 what the city is famous for
4 what you can see or do there

....
....
....
....
....
....
....
....

a ☐ **St Mark's Square, Venice**

b ☐ **the Rialto Bridge, Venice**

c ☐ **Gallerie dell'Accademia, Venice**

d ☐ **tourists on a gondola, Venice**

4 My place
We were staying in an apartment

VOCABULARY

1 Look at the pictures and write the words.

> apartment ~~beach~~ electricity market
> sand sink storm suitcase supper
> surfboard

1 .....beach.....

2 .....sand.....

3 .....surboard.....

4 .....supper.....

5 .....sutcase.....

6 .....sink.....

7 .....storm.....

8 .....market.....

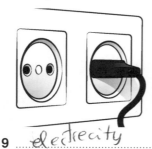

9 .....electricity.....

10 .....apartement.....

2 Now complete the email with the words from Exercise 1.

Hello Quique
How are you? Did I tell you about my holiday? It was terrible! We stayed in an **(1)** .....apartxment..... by the sea. On the first night there was a big **(2)** .....storm..... and we didn't have any **(3)** .....electricity..... for five hours. We had to have old cheese sandwiches for **(4)** .....supper..... Then Dad broke the **(5)** .....sink..... in the bathroom. I don't know how! The first day on the **(6)** .....beach..... was great. My sisters played on the **(7)** .....sand..... and I went surfing. But on the second day I lost my new **(8)** .....surboard..... I couldn't believe it.
We went to a street **(9)** .....market..... on our last morning. That was great. But on the way home Mum got off the train without her **(10)** .....suitcase..... All her new clothes were in it!
I hope your holiday was better than mine!
Carlos

9/10

GRAMMAR Past continuous and past simple

3 Match the two halves of the sentences.

1 I was making a sandwich   c
2 Juan was sending a text message   a
3 John was playing tennis   d
4 Jay and Nia were playing a video game online   e
5 Mary was running   b

a when his phone stopped working.
b when she hurt her toe.
c when I cut my finger.
d when he broke his racket.
e when the internet stopped working.

10/10

Plural → were

4 **Complete the sentences with the correct form of the verbs.**

0 I ...was reading... (read) a book about NASA when Kelly ...texted... (text) me.

1 Marta was ...swimming... (swim) when it ...started... (start) raining heavily.

2 Charlie was ...phoning/phoned... (phone) while you were ...playing... (play) football.

3 Dina was walking (walk) home from the sports club when she ...saw... (see) her French teacher Mr Roland.

4 Jim's mum ...was buying/bought... (bought) his birthday present while he was ...was playing... tennis at the club.

5 Sarah ...was watching... (watch) a film in the cinema when someone ...took... (take) her bag.

6 Bruna and I ...were flying... (fly) to London when the big storm ...came... (come).

7 It was very busy in our house at seven o'clock this morning. While I ...was making... (make) breakfast, my mother ...was talking... (talk) on the phone, my father ...was cleaning... (clean) the floor and my sisters ...were playing... (play) football with the dog.

8 Katie was ...doing... (do) her homework when her best friend ...arrived... (arrive) to see her.

14/15

5 👁 **Students often make mistakes with the past simple and past continuous. Correct the three underlined sentences in the email.**

Hi Henry
How are you? Thanks for your email.
I watched a great football match yesterday –
AC Milan against Inter Milan. Inter won 3–0.
(1) I was watching it with my family. We really enjoyed it.
After the match we had a party for my sister. It was her fifteenth birthday. At the party there were a lot of people. **(2)** We are dancing, eating and drinking. We had a great time.
You asked me about my holiday in Spain. Well, I enjoyed it very much. We did lots of things. We swam in the sea. We went for long walks. We played basketball. **(3)** We were lying on the beach every day. We ate meals in nice restaurants. I made friends with a boy and girl from Ireland.
Love
Petra

1 ...I watched...

2 ....

3 ....

WRITING

EXAM TIPS

Writing Part 7
- Always read the instructions and the example answer.
- Look at the words that go before and after each space. This will help you decide what kind of word goes in each space.

6 ⬤ **Complete Wojciech's blog. Write ONE word for each space.**

Example: | 0 | with |

I live in Krakow **(0)** ...with... my parents. We came here two years **(1)** ...ago.... It's a very beautiful city, perhaps the **(2)** ...most... beautiful one in Poland.
We live in an apartment in the centre **(3)** ...of... the city. It's only five minutes away **(4)** ...+)... a famous square, where you **(5)** ...can... buy postcards and many other things.

Our apartment is on the sixth floor and **(6)** ...the... building doesn't have a lift. The apartment is small, **(7)** ...but... we love it. **(8)** ...There... are five rooms: two bedrooms, a bathroom, a kitchen and a living room. **(9)** ...My... own bedroom has music posters **(10)** ...on... all the walls.
I'm very happy living here.

10/10

No two homes are the same

VOCABULARY

1 Find eight adjectives.

p	u	n	u	s	u	a	l	q	t
r	d	s	z	e	y	c	o	l	d
e	o	l	e	y	p	n	d	g	a
t	e	i	g	f	i	h	x	t	r
t	d	g	w	e	u	d	s	j	k
y	f	h	a	t	o	l	b	e	n
a	t	t	r	a	c	t	i	v	e
l	a	d	m	o	v	f	o	k	m

(handwritten list:) cold ✗ dark ✗ active warm ✗ slight light ✗ pretty old ✗ unusual

 *(handwritten 7/5)*

2 Now complete the sentences with the words from Exercise 1.

1 When our house is very ......active...... I always feel tired.

2 This knife is the most ......old / unusual / useful...... object in our house. We can use it for so many things.

3 It's so ......dark / old...... in my brother's house. He never turns the heating on! ......used unusual......

4 My friend lives in an ......old...... house. The bathroom and bedrooms are downstairs, and the living room and kitchen are upstairs.

5 It's always very ......cold light...... in our house because all the rooms have really big windows. We never turn the lamps on until the evening.

6 My grandparents live in a ......warm...... little house near a river.

7 My uncle and aunt's house is very ......light dark....... They have lamps on all the time – even in the summer!

8 My sister is painting her house yellow – she thinks it's a more ......pretty...... colour than brown.

LISTENING

3 ▶5 Listen to the description of an apartment in Paris. Match the rooms to the information.

1 living room   a doesn't have a window
2 dining room   b has a new mirror
3 bathroom   c has a new table
4 kitchen   d has a new carpet
5 bedroom   e has a view of the Eiffel Tower

4 ▶5 Listen again and answer the questions.

1 Which is the smallest room?

....

2 Which is the biggest room?

....

3 Which room has an old table?

....

4 Which room has an old mirror?

....

Prepare to write a description of a home

5 Read the descriptions. Replace the underlined words with the correct pronouns. Then match the descriptions to the houses.

1
My cousin lives there with her parents. Their home is very small. **(0)** <u>Their home</u> is not the best place for very tall people, but my cousin likes living there because **(1)** <u>my cousin</u> can travel and be at home at the same time.

2
My brother and his wife live on the top floor of an apartment block in Istanbul. **(2)** <u>My brother and his wife</u> really like their home. It's a beautiful apartment. **(3)** <u>The apartment</u> is very small, but you can see the Bosphorus and the Galata Bridge from the window.

3
My grandfather built the house thirty years ago in a forest. **(4)** <u>My grandfather</u> is very good at making things with his hands. My grandparents love living in the house. **(5)** <u>The house</u> is very quiet.

0 ....It.......
1 ....he/she.......
2 ....they.......
3 ....it.......
4 ....He.......
5 ....it.......

6 Now write a description of the home of someone you know. Use pronouns.

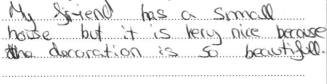

My friend has a small house but it is very nice because the decoration is so beautifull.

a **1**

b

c

5 School
Choose your topic carefully

GRAMMAR Comparative and superlative adverbs

1 Find the odd one out.

1 good	bad	easy	most quickly
2 more quickly	more easily	careful	better
3 badly	careful	well	quickly
4 best	worst	most carefully	quick
5 quickly	easily	carefully	more quickly
6 most easily	more quickly	more carefully	worse
7 more easily	more carefully	best	worse
8 badly	well	easily	better

2 Complete the table with the words from Exercise 1.

Adjective	Simple adverb	Comparative adverb	Superlative adverb
good	well	better	
....	....	worse	worst most quickly
....	....	....	....
....	easily	....	....
careful	....	....	....

3 Choose the right words to complete the sentences.

1 Mrs Black speaks *too quickly / more quickly* than the other teachers.
2 Toni plays basketball *the best / better* of all the players on our team.
3 Chris runs *more quickly / quickly* than Sam.
4 Nobody did well in the history exam, but I did *badly / worst* of all.
5 I can't hear you. You're speaking too *quiet / quietly.*
6 Mila does her homework *carefully / more carefully* than I do.

4 Read sentences 1–5. Are sentences a and b right (✔) or wrong (✗)?

1 Brian speaks more quickly than Gordon. Ronan speaks the most quickly.
   a Ronan speaks less quickly than Brian.
   b Gordon speaks less quickly than Brian.
2 Ruth reads less clearly than Sarah. Sarah reads less clearly than Jo.
   a Sarah reads more clearly than Ruth.
   b Jo reads the most clearly.
3 Nick drives more carefully than Ed. David drives the most carefully.
   a Ed drives less carefully than Nick.
   b Nick drives more carefully than David.
4 Emily makes friends less easily than George. George makes friends less easily than William.
   a William makes friends more easily than George.
   b Emily makes friends the most easily.

5 Complete the sentences with *more, most* or *less.*

1 I play football .... often than I did when I was a girl. I prefer watching football now.
2 Mr Sanchez explains things .... carefully than Mr Wright. I prefer Mr Sanchez!
3 My brother learns languages .... easily than I do. He can speak English, French and Russian.
4 Sara speaks the .... quickly of all the people in the class. I never understand what she says!
5 We visit my grandparents .... often than we did in the past because they live very far away.

6 👁 **Students often make mistakes with comparative and superlative adverbs. Correct the mistakes in two of these sentences. Three of the sentences are correct.**

1 I speak German better than my brother.

....

2 Every day at the college you learn lots of words in English and this helps you to speak English more easy.

....
....
....

3 Today is my birthday. Everyone gave me presents. The present I best like is the computer my parents gave me.

....
....
....

4 My father drives more carefully than my uncle.

....

5 Our Spanish teacher explains things more clearly than our French teacher.

....
....

VOCABULARY

7 **Look at the pictures and write the words.**

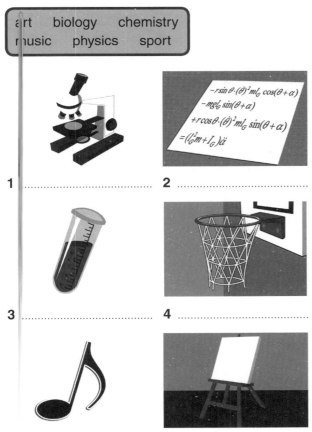

| art | biology | chemistry |
| music | physics | sport |

1 .... 2 ....

3 .... 4 ....

5 .... 6 ....

8 **Match the two halves of the sentences.**

1 The maths ....
2 We used ....
3 I passed ....
4 There were 50 ....
5 My friend failed ....
6 We took four ....
7 I've got a diploma ....
8 Our school uniform is ....

a students in the classroom.
b her history exam. She wasn't very happy.
c paper was the most difficult. I didn't understand all the questions.
d all my exams.
e dictionaries in our English exam.
f in Spanish from the University of Salamanca.
g horrible: blue trousers and green shirts.
h exams in two days. We were very tired. We do our fifth exam next week.

LISTENING

9 ▶6 **Listen to Mrs Ross talking to her class. Are the sentences right (✔) or wrong (✗)?**

1 She's the new chemistry teacher. ....
2 Her grandfather is from Scotland. ....
3 She went to Bristol University. ....
4 She was at university for four years. ....
5 She taught at the Science Academy for ten years. ....

10 ▶6 **Listen again and choose the right answer (a or b).**

1 Mrs Ross is from ....
   a England   b Scotland
2 She's .... years old.
   a forty-two   b fifty-four
3 She studied chemistry and .... at university.
   a biology   b physics
4 She .... watches TV on Sunday evenings.
   a usually   b sometimes

Home schooling

VOCABULARY

1 Complete the text with the words in the box.

| computer programs | home school | miss | models | parents | study |

My uncle and aunt (1) .... my cousins. My cousins love it. They say they don't (2) .... their friends from school.

My cousins' (3) .... are both teachers, so they think carefully about the lessons. My cousins know exactly what they are doing and why they are doing it. My cousins (4) .... all the normal subjects like maths and English, but they also do lots of other things as well. They write (5) .... and make (6) .... of railways and bridges. This helps them understand how things work. I think my cousins are very lucky.

2 Read the sentences. Match the meanings of *take* to the verbs in the box.

| carry | catch | ~~do~~ | go along | make | use |

0	I have to take my geography exam again.	.........do.........
1	We're going to take a train to Edinburgh in the morning.	....
2	Take an umbrella. It's going to rain later.	....
3	I should take some medicine because I've got a bad cold.	....
4	Take the first turning on the left. The cinema is on the right.	....
5	My father always takes lots of photographs on holiday.	....

READING

EXAM TIPS

Reading Part 3b
- Read the instructions and look at the example answer.
- Read the whole conversation once before you choose your answers so that you know what it is about.

3 🔘 **Complete the conversation between two friends. What does Luke say to Claire? For each question, write the correct letter A–H in the space.**

Example:
Claire: What's your new school like, Luke?
Luke: 0 ...G....
Claire: Really? How many are there?
Luke: 1 ....
Claire: That's a lot. Do the teachers give you homework every night?
Luke: 2 ....
Claire: Lucky you! And what's your uniform like?
Luke: 3 ....
Claire: I suppose it's OK, but we miss you, Luke.
Luke: 4 ....
Claire: Great, he's the best teacher.
Luke: 5 ....
Claire: The big, black one? All the time!

A I agree. Is he still wearing that hat?
B Good idea! I miss his lessons.
C Do you? How's Mr Yarn, by the way?
D When I started last week, it was.
E Only three times a week, actually.
F I'm not sure. About 1,000, I think.
G It's great! There are lots of students.
H Not bad, it's green and grey. Anyway, how's my old school?

WRITING

4 **Match the phrases to the information.**

1 Hi / Hello / Dear ....
2 How are you? / Thanks for your email.   ....
3 Email me soon. / Send me an email soon.   ....
4 Love / Bye / Best wishes   ....

a ending an email
b beginning an email
c first sentences in an email
d last sentences in an email

5 **Complete the email with the verbs in the box.**

| are | have | had | passed | started | studying |

Hi Marco
How are you? I'm OK. I **(1)** .... at my new
school last month. It's very big. There **(2)** ....
2,000 students at the school. We **(3)** ....
to wear a purple uniform. It's horrible! We have lots
of homework every night, but our holidays are long.
We have two months in the summer!
I'm **(4)** .... lots of new subjects. My favourite
is German. It's difficult, but I really like it. Last week we
(5) .... exams. I **(6)** .... them all.
I hope everything is OK at your school.
Email me soon.
Love
Silvia

6 **You are Marco. Write an email to Silvia. Use the phrases from Exercise 4 and this information:**

size of school:	small, 300 students
uniform:	no uniform
homework:	only at the weekend
holidays:	short, four weeks in the summer
subjects:	favourite subject is science

....
....
....
....
....
....
....

6 It's very special
It belongs to a friend of mine

VOCABULARY

1 Use the words in the box to answer the questions.

> glass   gold   leather   plastic   silver
> wood   wool

1 Which two materials come from animals?

.... , ...

2 Which material do we use to make paper?

....

3 Which two materials do we use to make expensive necklaces and rings?

.... , ...

4 Which material do we use to make mirrors?

....

5 Which material do we use to make bags for supermarkets?

....

2 Are the sentences right (✔) or wrong (✗)?

1 Shoes are never made of leather.   ....

2 Envelopes are always made of wool.   ....

3 Lots of tables and chairs are made of wood.   ....

4 Jumpers are usually made of paper.   ....

5 Bottles are often made of plastic.   ....

3 Match the two halves of the sentences.

1 My uncle and aunt live in an   ....

2 These shoes are   ....

3 My pillows feel so   ....

4 Your scarf is   ....

5 My mother gave me this lovely necklace   ....

a soft. I love sleeping on them!

b old house next to the sea.

c so small. I wore them when I was a boy.

d when I was a little girl.

e really pretty. Where did you buy it?

4 Read the completed sentences in Exercise 3 and complete these sentences.

1 ......*Small*...... and .... are the opposite of 'big'.

2 We use .... and .... to say that objects are nice to look at.

3 The opposite of 'new' is ....

4 The opposite of 'hard' is ....

GRAMMAR   Possession

5 Look at the pictures. Which sentence is right (✔)?

0 Who does the guitar belong to?

a It's my friend's.

b It's my friends'.   ....

1 Who does the cat belong to?

a It's my cousins'.   ....

b It's my cousin's.   ....

2 Who does the computer belong to?

a It belongs to friends of his.   ....

b It belongs to a friend of theirs.   ....

3 Who does the necklace belong to?

a It's their daughters'.   ....

b It's their daughter's.   ....

6 Choose the right word to complete the sentences.

1 Don't touch that. It's *my / mine*.
2 That's his suitcase and those are *their / theirs* suitcases.
3 Helen, I've got *yours / your* video game.
4 I've got one brother. My *brother's / brothers'* name is Fabio.
5 This jumper is his and that one is *yours / your*.
6 These surfboards are *our / ours*. Those ones are yours.
7 Are these shoes *her / hers*? Or are they his?

7 Students often make mistakes with possessive pronouns, possessive determiners and the possessive *'s*. Correct the mistakes in these sentences.

1 I watched a volleyball's game last Friday.
....
2 The colour of mine bedroom is blue.
....
3 I bought a smartphone. You can take great photos with it's camera.
....
....
4 I went to the football match with my father and two friends of us.
....
....
5 I bought a pair of jeans because mines are small.
....

LISTENING

8 ▶7 Listen to the conversation between Alex and Jane. Match the people to the objects.

1 Daniel
2 Ryan
3 George
4 Alex
5 Jane

a book
b mobile phone
c keys
d video games
e tennis racket

9 ▶7 Listen to the conversation again. Who says what? Write *J* for Jane and *A* for Alex.

1 That's all right. ....
2 Moving house is really boring. ....
3 Can I have a look at it? ....
4 Is it yours? ....
5 Oh, they're mine. ....

READING

Hans Sloane

The most important person in the early history of the British Museum wasn't English or Scottish, but an Irish doctor called Hans Sloane. Hans was born in 1660. After he studied in England and France, he worked in London as a doctor. He met many people there.

In 1687 he travelled to Jamaica and learned about its animals and plants. Many years later he wrote books about his adventures in that country. In Jamaica Hans was given drinking chocolate with water. He didn't like it, but when he got back to London, he mixed the chocolate with milk. Hans didn't make much money from his books, but he made a lot from the new milk chocolate drink. Years after his death a company called Cadbury started producing it.

Hans was a good doctor and he enjoyed meeting important people in London, but collecting things was his favourite thing to do. During his life, he collected 71,000 objects: mainly plants and animals, books, coins and medals. Hans wanted these things to be in one place where many different people could look at them.

When Hans died, his family sold the objects to King George II. The king gave them to the British Museum in 1753. Four years later, George II gave his collection of books to the museum, and in 1759 people visited it for the first time.

1 🔘 **Read the article about a man called Hans Sloane. For questions 1–7 choose A, B or C.**

Example:

0 Hans Sloane was from
  A Scotland.　　　　　　**B** England　　　　　　Ⓒ Ireland.

1 What did Hans do in France?
  A He was a student.　　**B** He met many people there.　**C** He worked as a doctor.

2 What did Hans do in Jamaica?
  A He wrote about his adventures.　**B** He studied different things.　**C** He read books.

3 When Hans returned to England, what did he do with the drinking chocolate?
  A He left it in Jamaica.　**B** He added water to it.　**C** He put milk in it.

4 Hans made a lot of money from
  A his books.　　**B** a milk chocolate drink.　**C** plants and animals.

5 Hans most enjoyed
  A meeting important people.　**B** looking at things.　**C** collecting objects.

6 Who sold Hans's collection of objects?
  A Hans's family　　**B** King George II　　**C** Hans

7 When did people first go to the British Museum?
  A in 1753　　　　**B** in 1757　　　　**C** in 1759

VOCABULARY

2 Find four adjectives, a verb and a noun.

r	p	o	s	s	i	b	l	e
h	e	i	o	l	e	o	z	c
o	g	c	f	d	l	n	h	a
b	d	h	e	u	g	j	x	r
b	t	n	r	i	c	h	e	e
y	r	c	k	w	v	n	l	f
a	i	f	j	m	y	e	b	u
w	o	n	d	e	r	f	u	l

Prepare to write adjective order

4 Choose the right words to complete the sentences. Then match the sentences to the pictures.

1 My brother's favourite thing is his *big white /
white big* computer.
2 My mother loves her *old black / black old* car.
3 My sister's got a *gold wonderful / wonderful
gold* ring.
4 My grandfather lives in a *little round / round
little* house by the sea.
5 I've got a *lovely wooden / wooden lovely* box.
6 I've got lots of *gold small / small gold* coins.

3 Now complete the sentences with the words from Exercise 1. Use the past simple form of the verb.

1 My brother .... some money for
finding a gold necklace and three beautiful rings.
2 Is it .... to visit the Guggenheim
Museum in Bilbao on Mondays?
3 Please be .... with that bowl.
It's very old.
4 My uncle sold his paintings to a
.... businesswoman from Berlin.
5 London has lots of museums. My favourite
is the Science Museum. I think it's
.... !
6 My sister's .... is collecting old
bowls from around the world.

5 Complete the sentences with the pairs of adjectives in the box.

amazing leather   beautiful silver
big wooden   old black

1 My brother loves our .... dog.
2 What's your favourite thing? That's easy! It's
our .... tree house!
3 My sister loves her ....
necklace. It's her favourite thing in the world.
4 My cousin's favourite object is his
.... belt!

6 Describe three objects that are important to you. Use pairs of adjectives.

....
....
....
....
....
....
....
....

7 Travel and holidays
We're climbing next week

VOCABULARY

1 Complete the activity words.

1 _ l _ m b _ _ _ _   2 _ i k _ _ g   3 _ _ _ _ n t _ _ n b _ _ i _ _   4 _ i _ _ i r _ n _

2 Match the phrasal verbs to the definitions.

1 get back   **a** wake up and get out of bed
2 get lost   **b** go onto a bus, train, plane or boat
3 get on   **c** travel to a place
4 get to   **d** not know where you are
5 get up   **e** return from somewhere to a place you were before

3 Complete the conversation with the correct form of the phrasal verbs from Exercise 2.

Carla: How are you **(1)** .... Edinburgh?

Marko: By train. We've got to **(2)** .... really early tomorrow morning. We're **(3)** .... the train at 5.30.

Carla: That's very early, Marko.

Marko: I know. We'll be tired. I hope we don't **(4)** .... on the way to the train station.

Carla: When are you **(5)** .... ?

Marko: On Monday evening at about seven o'clock.

Carla: Well, have a great time this weekend. Edinburgh is a lovely city!

GRAMMAR   Present continuous for future

4 What is everyone doing on Saturday? Complete the sentences with the present continuous form of the verbs. Then match the sentences to the pictures.

1 Laura .... (meet) her mum in a café.
2 Stefan and his dad .... (play) tennis.
3 I .... (study) Chinese.
4 We .... (take) our brother to the zoo.
5 Lucinda .... (have) a birthday party.
6 Eliot .... (visit) his grandparents.

5 Put the words in the right order to make sentences.

0 flying / 10th / of / we're / the / to / Mexico / on / May

...We're flying to Mexico on the 10th of May.

1 my / grandparents / for / July / the / on / 16th / lunch / meeting / I'm / of

....

....

2 having / my / of / they're / party / on / baby cousin / the / a / 3rd / November / for

....

....

3 doing / last / 22nd / English / on / June / exam / my / of / the / I'm

....

....

4 visiting / sister / my / the / in / 12th / on / of / Rio / we're / October

....

....

5 parents / me / theatre / to / the / taking / on / March / 23rd / my / are / of / the

....

....

6 Write four sentences about things you and your family are doing this year. Use the present continuous and a date.

0 ...Gonzalo and I are playing in a table tennis competition on the 4th of June.

1 ....

....

2 ....

....

3 ....

....

4 ....

....

7 Students often make mistakes with the present continuous for the future. Correct the mistakes in these sentences.

1 I'm going to the airport. My mum arrive at 3.30 pm.

....

....

2 My father's getting us to the sports centre at six o'clock. Don't forget to bring your racket!

....

....

3 Would you like to help me paint my bedroom? We starting on Sunday morning at 10 am.

....

....

4 My friend Jacek is from Poland. Next week he come to see us in England.

....

....

5 Don't forget we meet at 3 pm at my house.

....

....

LISTENING

EXAM TIPS

Listening Part 5
- Never leave an empty space. Always write something.
- Always check your spelling and write numbers in figures not words

8 ● ▶8 You will hear some information about a trip. Listen and complete each question.

Today's trip

Name of the Island: ..Dolphin Island..

Time to leave hotel: **(1)** ....

What to bring: **(2)** ....

Place to have lunch: **(3)** ....

Woodside Castle

When it was built: **(4)** ....

Things to see: **(5)** ... clothes, furniture and ....

I'd prefer to visit the Arctic

VOCABULARY

1 **Put the letters in order to make words for ways of travelling.**

1 s i p h ....
2 a b o t ....
3 o e o t r s c ....
4 f t o o ....
5 i c o h e l p r t e ....
6 r m a t ....
7 k m o e i t o r b ....
8 d u n u g d e o r r n ....

2 **Complete the sentences with words from Exercise 1. Use the plural form if necessary.**

1 A .... is a small motorbike. They are popular in big cities.

2 .... are usually found in cities. They use electricity and move along special metal lines in the road.

3 A very large boat is called a ....

4 If we walk somewhere, we can say we 'go on ....'.

5 In many cities in the world the .... is called the metro.

6 At the weekend we flew in a .... It was great! Do you know how they fly? They've got special parts on top of them called 'blades'. They go round and round really fast!

READING

3 **Complete the text with prepositions and articles.**

Hi Paula

I'm glad you had **(1)** .... good time on holiday. We went to Italy last year. It's great, isn't it?

We're going **(2)** .... holiday next week, actually. Dad really liked the idea of Spain, but Mum preferred Portugal. They asked me to choose. 'OK,' I said. 'France.'

We're going to stay in **(3)** .... small hotel. Dad wanted to go camping, but Mum doesn't enjoy that type of holiday. **(4)** .... hotel is near the sea. It's famous for its restaurant too.

But I don't really like holidays. You work hard **(5)** .... 50 weeks a year and then worry **(6)** .... your holiday. My parents are worrying about everything at the moment: packing clothes, finding passports, buying suntan lotion, choosing books to read. This is why I think the perfect holiday is staying at home and doing nothing. Anyway, I'll call you when we come back.

Love
Luke

4 **Read the email again. Are the sentences right (✔) or wrong (✗)?**

1 Paula went on holiday to Spain. ....
2 Luke's dad wanted to go on holiday to Portugal. ....
3 Luke's going on holiday to France. ....
4 Luke isn't going camping. ....
5 Luke enjoys holidays. ....

WRITING

5 Complete the blog with the words in the box.

> are   built   driving   getting   reading   takes   talk

HARRY'S HAPPY HOLIDAY BLOG

We're going to Peru tomorrow! My parents **(1)** .... very excited, but the most excited person in our family is my little sister, Emily. It's the only thing she wants to **(2)** .... about! Emily's **(3)** .... a big book on Peru at the moment. 'Harry, Harry,' she says, 'can I tell you about the Incas, please? They were amazing people! They **(4)** .... Machu Picchu! Are we going there, Harry?'

We're **(5)** .... to Peru by plane. The flight **(6)** .... about eight or nine hours, I think. Tomorrow will be a very long day. We're getting up at 2 am and then **(7)** .... to Heathrow airport near London. Our flight is at 8 am.

When we get to Peru, we're going to stay in a beautiful old city called Cuzco. Emily is going to tell me all about it!

We're coming back in two weeks' time, but I don't want to think about that yet!

6 Read the blog again and answer the questions.

1 Where is Harry going?

....

2 When is Harry going?

....

3 Who is Harry going with?

....

4 How is Harry getting there?

....

5 When is Harry coming back?

....

7 Now write about a future holiday.
Answer these questions:

1 Where are you going?
2 When are you going?
3 Who are you going with?
4 How are you getting there?
5 When are you coming back?

....
....
....
....
....
....
....
....

8 Life in the future
Will homes change in 20 years?

VOCABULARY

1 Put the letters in the right order to make words for things in the home.

1 riahc ....
2 fsoa ....
3 plam ....
4 sawginh camenih ....
5 degfir ....
6 kins ....
7 bardpocu ....

2 Look at the picture. Write the words from Exercise 1.

1 ....
2 ....
3 ....
4 ....
5 ....
6 ....
7 ....

3 Complete the text with the words in the box.

> electricity   furniture   garage   heating
> lights

We're going to move house next week. Today we packed everything in our old house. We've got a lot of (1) .... and it's heavy! I went up and down the stairs a hundred times.
Our new house has a really big (2) .... That's great because there is space in it for Mum's car and Dad's motorbike. But there are some problems with the new house at the moment. There is no (3) .... , so it's very cold.
And we lost the (4) .... in the kitchen yesterday, so none of the (5) .... in there are working!

GRAMMAR   Future with *will*

4 Put the words in the right order to make sentences and questions.

1 I / to the cinema / I'll go / don't think / with them

....

2 win / the Champions League / will / Chelsea

.... ?

3 will / the weather / get better / I think

....

4 Chris / do you think / his history exam / will pass

.... ?

5 won't win / our team / the Championship

....

6 be very different / will life / in the future

.... ?

5 Complete the sentences with the future form of the verbs.

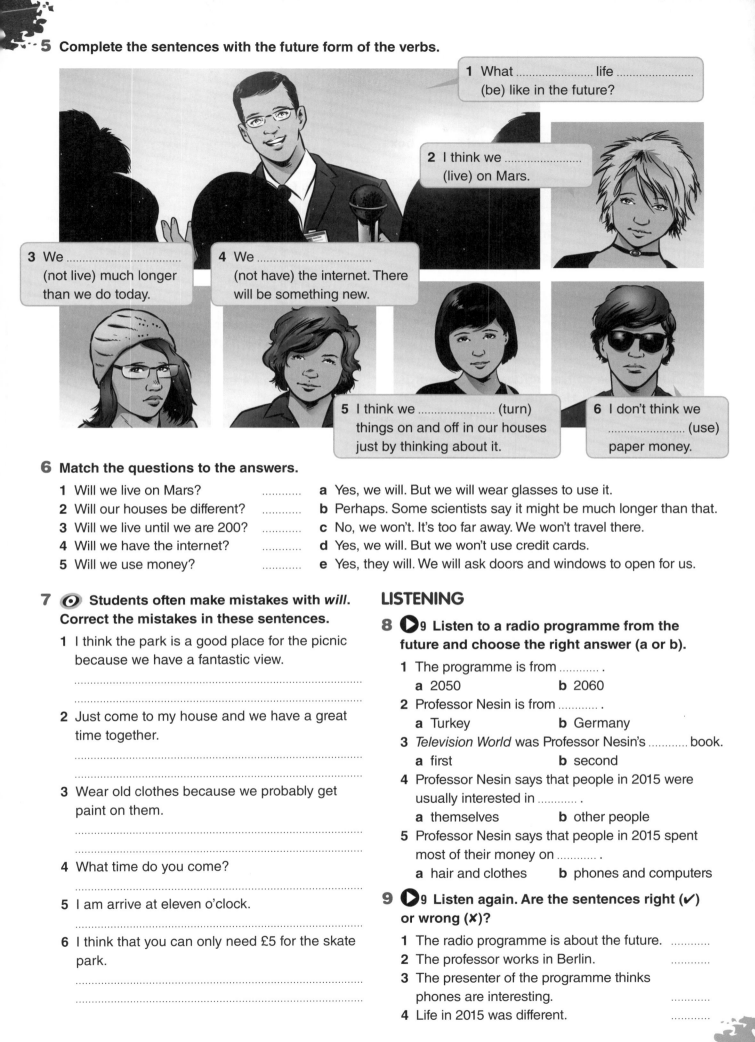

1 What .... life .... (be) like in the future?

2 I think we .... (live) on Mars.

3 We .... (not live) much longer than we do today.

4 We .... (not have) the internet. There will be something new.

5 I think we .... (turn) things on and off in our houses just by thinking about it.

6 I don't think we .... (use) paper money.

6 Match the questions to the answers.

1 Will we live on Mars?   ....
2 Will our houses be different? ....
3 Will we live until we are 200? ....
4 Will we have the internet?   ....
5 Will we use money?   ....

a Yes, we will. But we will wear glasses to use it.
b Perhaps. Some scientists say it might be much longer than that.
c No, we won't. It's too far away. We won't travel there.
d Yes, we will. But we won't use credit cards.
e Yes, they will. We will ask doors and windows to open for us.

7 👁 Students often make mistakes with *will*. Correct the mistakes in these sentences.

1 I think the park is a good place for the picnic because we have a fantastic view.
   ....
   ....

2 Just come to my house and we have a great time together.
   ....
   ....

3 Wear old clothes because we probably get paint on them.
   ....
   ....

4 What time do you come?
   ....

5 I am arrive at eleven o'clock.
   ....

6 I think that you can only need £5 for the skate park.
   ....
   ....

LISTENING

8 ▶9 Listen to a radio programme from the future and choose the right answer (a or b).

1 The programme is from ....
   a 2050   b 2060
2 Professor Nesin is from ....
   a Turkey   b Germany
3 *Television World* was Professor Nesin's .... book.
   a first   b second
4 Professor Nesin says that people in 2015 were usually interested in ....
   a themselves   b other people
5 Professor Nesin says that people in 2015 spent most of their money on ....
   a hair and clothes   b phones and computers

9 ▶9 Listen again. Are the sentences right (✔) or wrong (✗)?

1 The radio programme is about the future.   ....
2 The professor works in Berlin.   ....
3 The presenter of the programme thinks phones are interesting.   ....
4 Life in 2015 was different.   ....

What will we write?

VOCABULARY

1 Complete the table with the words in the box. Put the words in more than one column.

| book | kind | letter | picture | ring | watch |

Verbs	Nouns	Adjectives
....	....	....
....	....	
....	....	
	....	
	....	
	....	

2 Complete the conversations with the words from Exercise 1. Use the same word twice. Change the form of some of the words if necessary.

1 A: What .... of chocolate would you like from the supermarket, Grandma: white or dark?

   B: Oh, dark, please. Thank you for going to the shop for me, Tanya. You're so ....

2 A: I had a .... from the doctor, but I couldn't read it.

   B: Why not?

   A: The .... were too small.

3 A: I read in my .... about Milan that Giacomo is one of the best restaurants in the city, so I .... a table for us.

   B: Great! What time are we going?

4 A: I was .... TV last night when I saw an advert for a new .... If you ask it the time, it tells you.

   B: Wow, that's amazing!

5 A: We'll .... you when your .... is ready, Miss Jenson.

   B: Thank you very much.

6 A: Did you draw that .... ? Can I take a .... of it with my phone?

   B: Of course you can!

WRITING

EXAM TIPS

Writing Part 6
- Don't worry if you don't know an answer immediately. Move on to the next question and then go back to the one you thought was difficult.
- Answers can be singular or plural. Read the descriptions carefully to decide if the word needs to be in the plural form.

3 🔴 Read the descriptions of some things you find in the home. What is the word for each one? The first letter is already there. There is one space for each other letter in the word.

Example:

0 You can boil or fry your food on top of this. c o o k e r

1 This is a long comfortable seat for two people or more. s _ _ _

2 You go to sleep in this place. b _ _ _ _ _ _

3 This is often on a wall and tells you the time. c _ _ _ _ _

4 You can keep your car in this building. g _ _ _ _ _

5 You wash and shower in this place. b _ _ _ _ _ _ _

Prepare to write too, also, as well

4 Which pair of sentences is right (✔)?

1 a We will live on Mars. We will live on the Moon also. ....

   b We will live on Mars. We will also live on the Moon. ....

2 a We will wear glasses to use the internet. We will too have it in the walls of our houses. ....

   b We will wear glasses to use the internet. We will have it in the walls of our houses too. ....

3 a We will live until we are 150. We will be very active and healthy as well. ....

   b We will live until we are 150. We will as well be very active and healthy. ....

5 Complete the article with *too, also* and *as well*.

Life in the future

Where will we live?
What will life be like in the future? Nobody knows, of course, but I think lots of people will live in houses on the Moon. They will **(1)** .... live underground, but they won't live near the sea.

How will we travel?
Transport always changes, so I don't think there will be any cars in the future. People will travel everywhere in small planes instead. They will walk and cycle more **(2)** ....

What languages will we speak?
English won't be the world language in the future. People will speak Chinese instead. I think lots more people will speak Spanish and Arabic **(3)** ....

6 What will the future be like? Answer the questions. Use *I think, will/won't, too, also* and *as well*.

1 Where will we live?
2 How will we travel?
3 What languages will we speak?

....
....
....
....
....
....
....
....

9 Sport and games
They must do it for three months

VOCABULARY

1 Read about people's hobbies. Choose the right word.

I go every Friday. I love going! We learn salsa and tango. It's so much fun.

1 Ursula: dance classes / fitness classes

Doing this teaches me a lot about life. I practise every day. I want to be a black belt!

2 Toni: diving / karate

You have to think a lot about what you're doing. You only need one other person to play.

3 Eren: chess / fishing

My parents don't like me playing them. They say: 'Why don't you go outside and play football?'

4 Alistair: puzzles / video games

I do this every winter with my family. Last December I broke my leg doing it!

5 Andrey: climbing / skiing

I play this with my cousin every time we visit him in England! One player throws the ball and the other player tries to hit the ball with a bat.

6 Vladimir: cricket / golf

I really enjoy playing racket sports. That's why I started doing this.

7 Raúl: badminton / skateboarding

GRAMMAR *must, mustn't, have to, don't have to*

2 Match the two halves of the sentences.

1 We mustn't
2 We don't have to
3 You mustn't
4 I must get
5 You have to
6 You must tidy your room,

a eat all that cake, Artur. You'll feel sick.
b Robbie – your clothes are all over the floor.
c wear our uniform next Friday because it's the last day of school.
d use our mobile phones in school.
e a card for my grandfather. It's his birthday on Saturday.
f fill in a form before you can join the sports club.

3 Choose the right words to complete the sentences.

1 In our school, we *must / mustn't* wear our uniform all the time. We mustn't wear jeans or T-shirts.
2 We *have to / don't have to* walk in the corridor. We mustn't run.
3 We *don't have to / mustn't* talk in the classroom. We have to be quiet.
4 We *have to / don't have to* turn our mobile phones off when we go into the classroom. We mustn't use them in the class.

4 **What are the rules in your school? Write five rules. Use *must*, *mustn't* and *have to*.**

Our school **rules**

1 ....
2 ....
3 ....
4 ....
5 ....

5 **Students often make mistakes with *must*, *mustn't, have to* and *don't have to*. Correct the mistakes in three of these sentences. Which two sentences are correct?**

1 You have not to bring anything because the teacher will give you what you need.

....
....

2 It will be cold, so you must wear warm clothes!

....
....

3 You mustn't spend so much time on the internet.

....
....

4 Tomorrow night you must come to my house. To get to my house you had to take the 15 bus.

....
....

5 You don't must bring anything because I've got everything.

....
....

LISTENING

EXAM TIPS

Listening Part 3
• You hear each recording in the listening exam twice. Use the second time you listen to check your answers.
• You will hear all three answers in the conversation, but only one of them is right. Listen carefully.

6 ⏺ ▶10 **Listen to Matt talking to Emma about his basketball class. For each question, choose the right answer (A, B or C).**

Example:
0 The basketball class is on
  A Tuesdays.
  (**B**) Wednesdays.
  C Thursdays.

1 If you pay for one class at a time, it costs
  A £10.
  B £15.
  C £50.

2 The basketball teacher is from
  A Scotland.
  B Mexico.
  C England.

3 Which place is closest to the sports centre?
  A the library.
  B the swimming pool.
  C the cinema.

4 What does Emma have to wear at the class?
  A trainers
  B a T-shirt
  C shorts

5 To join the class, students must
  A visit the website.
  B fill in a form.
  C bring a letter from their parents.

Are they really sports?

VOCABULARY

1 Choose the right word to complete the sentences.

1 My parents gave me a beautiful chess *set / match* for my birthday.
2 I love playing board *games / competitions* with my family.
3 My sister is very good at card *matches / games*.
4 I would like to win a gold *medal / circle* at the Olympic Games.

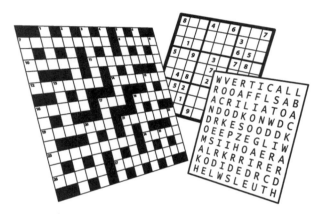

2 Complete the blog with the plural form of the words in the box.

fan	match	prize	puzzle	winner

THE BIG PUZZLE

Everyone in my school loves football. They're all **(1)** .... of Manchester United or Arsenal or Chelsea. Every Monday morning they talk about the most important **(2)** .... of the weekend. 'We're the **(3)** .... ,' they shout if their team wins. They don't say much if their team loses. I don't know why they love football so much. Nobody gives them anything for it. The players get all the money and all the **(4)** .... No, I don't like football. I prefer doing **(5)** ....

READING

3 Choose the right words to complete the text.

(1) *In / On* 2013 Magnus Carlsen became the world chess champion. He was only 22 years old and won against Viswanathan Anand in the final. Anand **(2)** *is / was* the world champion in 2000, 2007, 2008, 2010 and 2012, so it wasn't easy for Magnus to win.

Magnus was born in Norway, but he and his family lived in Finland for a long time. While the family were living in Finland, Magnus's father taught **(3)** *he / him* to play chess. Magnus started playing when he was **(4)** *only / ever* five years old. Thinking carefully is very important in chess. And when Magnus was a boy, he could already do that **(5)** *with / for* a long time. Magnus learned quickly and by the time he was thirteen years old, he was **(6)** *a / an* excellent player. He won **(7)** *lot / lots* of competitions when he was a teenager.

The Russian chess player Garry Kasparov, who was the best player in **(8)** *the / a* world in the 1980s **(9)** *and / or* 1990s, calls Magnus 'the Harry Potter of chess'.

4 Read the text again. Are the sentences right (✔) or wrong (✗)?

1 Viswanathan Anand didn't win the World Championship in 2013. ....
2 Magnus Carlsen was a teenager when he started playing chess. ....
3 Magnus was born in Finland. ....
4 When Magnus was thirteen, he was able to play chess very well. ....
5 People call Garry Kasparov 'the Harry Potter of chess'. ....

WRITING

5 Choose the right words to complete the text. Then number the paragraphs in the right order.

A Year in Sport

BLOG   ABOUT ME   SEARCH

Tennis and Rafa

a ☐ Of course, I'm not one of the best players in the history of the sport. I only play in the summer, and I'm not very good at it. I always play against my best friend from school. He usually wins. I **(1)** *don't have to | must* try harder to win!

b ☐ But the most interesting thing about a tennis match isn't how long it might be, but how it can change so quickly. You have to think very carefully about what you're doing, and you also **(2)** *have to | don't have to* be ready to move very fast. You need to be very fit to play the sport well. You **(3)** *have to | don't have to* be very tall, but it can help your serve if you are!

c ☐ I enjoy watching lots of different sports, but my favourite sport is tennis. I like it because you never know how long matches will take. Sometimes, players only play for an hour and a half. At other times, they **(4)** *have to | don't have to* play for four or five hours. The longest match in tennis history took eleven hours and five minutes!

d ☐ But the most interesting players can do more than serve fast. Players like Rafa Nadal – he's my favourite. I like Rafa because he really wants to win, and he works so hard. Rafa teaches people an important message – you **(5)** *have to | mustn't* stop trying. I think he is one of the best players in the history of tennis.

6 Write about a sport that you like. Answer these questions:

1 What is the name of the sport?
2 Why do you like it?
3 Which stars of the sport do you like?
4 Do you play this sport?

....
....
....
....
....
....
....
....

10 Useful websites
Problems, problems

VOCABULARY

1 **Complete the sentences with the words in the box. Use the plural form if necessary.**

> contact   guest   member   neighbour

1 Last week our new .... moved in next door to us. They're from Hungary. They're teaching me some Hungarian words!
2 Do you have to pay to be a .... of the online film club you told me about?
3 My parents are having .... tonight. Two old friends of theirs from university are coming to our house for dinner.
4 How many .... do you have in your phone?

2 **Choose the right word (a or b) to complete the sentences.**

1 He's a really .... friend. We talk on the phone every day.
   a new   **b** close
2 She .... the sports club last month. She goes there three times a week.
   a joined   **b** left
3 I don't have his number in my phone, so I can't .... him.
   a write   **b** contact
4 She loves .... new people. She's so friendly.
   a missing   **b** meeting
5 He .... friends so easily. He talks to everyone.
   a invites   **b** makes
6 My best friend moved to a new school last month. I really .... him.
   a make   **b** miss
7 I .... too many people to my birthday party.
   a invited   **b** joined
8 Sara and Jane are .... friends of my mum's. They met twenty years ago!
   a old   **b** new

GRAMMAR   Verb patterns – gerunds and infinitives

3 **Choose the right word to complete the sentences.**

1 I finished *doing* / *to do* my homework and I went to the cinema.
2 My sister enjoys *to play* / *playing* the piano.
3 I need *to learn* / *learning* computer code because I want to create my own website.
4 My friend wanted *to buy* / *buying* a laptop, but they were too expensive.
5 Jack doesn't mind *studying* / *study* for exams, but Ronnie hates it.
6 My brother hopes *to become* / *becoming* a photographer.

4 **Complete the sentences with the gerund (*going*) or the infinitive (*to go*) form of the verbs.**

1 I hope .... (live) in New York when I leave school.
2 Sara doesn't mind .... (see) the film again.
3 You need .... (study) really hard if you want to do well in your exams.
4 I'm worried about .... (move) to a new city.
5 My sister decided .... (go) to university in Istanbul.

5 Match the two halves of the sentences

1 I tried to
2 My brother loves
3 I started
4 I'm thinking of
5 My sister hopes to
6 Jay's worried about

a playing that new video game last night. I thought it was really difficult!
b failing his maths exam. He says he needs to study more.
c play for the school basketball team next year.
d make a pizza for my family, but it didn't go very well. It was horrible!
e meeting his friends at the weekend. They always have a really good time.
f studying Russian next term. Mrs Smith says we can choose between Russian and French.

6 Students often make mistakes with gerunds and infinitives. Which sentence is right (✔)?

1 a I'm not very interested in seeing this film. ....
  b I'm not very interested in see this film. ....
2 a The class starts on Monday. Don't forget to bring your things. ....
  b The class starts on Monday. Don't forget bring your things. ....
3 a I like reading and listening to music. Swim is also good. ....
  b I like reading and listening to music. Swimming is also good. ....
4 a Thank you very much for invite me to your party. ....
  b Thank you very much for inviting me to your party. ....
5 a At the music club we sing and learn to play the guitar. ....
  b At the music club we sing and learn playing the guitar. ....

READING

EXAM TIPS

Reading Part 3a
- Read each sentence carefully before you look at the answers.
- Think about the conversations you have every day. They include the kind of questions and sentences you will see in this part of the Reading exam.

7 Complete the five conversations. For each question, choose A, B, or C.

Example:
0 I can't come to the park, sorry.
  A What about you?   B What fun!
  Ⓒ What a pity.
1 I'm interested in films.
  A Of course not!   B A little bit.
  C Me too!
2 Could you close the door?
  A Sure.   B I hope not.
  C I'm all right, thanks.
3 What was the book like?
  A I think it was.   B Really exciting.
  C Yes, I know!
4 Why don't we go to the pool tomorrow?
  A That's right.   B Yes, we do.
  C OK, I'd like that.
5 Look at that dog!
  A Is it Sara's?   B I liked it.
  C John did it.

I love using this website

VOCABULARY

1 Choose the right words to complete the sentences.

1 Click on the *link / menu* to find out more about saving the planet.
2 The *web / blog* was invented by Tim Berners-Lee in 1989.
3 Amazon is a very popular *site / message board*.
4 My sister writes a really interesting *blog / menu* about video games.
5 There are lots of pages on the site, so use the *menu / web* to help you find the page you want.
6 My brother likes writing comments on *message boards / links*.

2 Find six internet verbs.

s	r	u	p	l	o	a	d
p	a	z	n	t	g	k	q
o	b	v	i	w	v	m	p
s	x	s	e	a	r	c	h
t	r	e	c	o	r	d	k
d	o	w	n	l	o	a	d

3 Complete the sentences with the correct form of the verbs from Exercise 2.

1 I forgot to .... the file and lost all my homework.
2 Chiara .... her songs to YouTube last week and now she's got a lot of fans of her music.
3 Yuri .... messages online twenty or thirty times a week.
4 We .... a great new film onto my computer last night. We're going to watch it this weekend.
5 Bartek's band .... a new song the other day. They're going to put it on their website.
6 I usually find what I'm looking for when I .... for it online.

LISTENING

4 ▶11 Listen to Stuart talking to Cathy about a music website and choose the right answer (a or b).

1 The music on the website is ....
   a old   b new
2 The site is ....
   a British   b American
3 There are .... songs on the site.
   a 10,000   b 100,000
4 You .... upload songs to the site.
   a can   b can't
5 Cathy .... record an album.
   a wants to   b doesn't want to

Prepare to write a description of a website

5 Choose the right words to complete the sentences. Then write the websites with the descriptions.

> Amazon   Facebook   Skype   YouTube

1 ....
   This / These website is a great place to find books, music and DVDs. I buy eBooks from it with my birthday money.

2 ....
   I use this site to make calls. You *can / can't* call anywhere in the world for free! I speak to my grandparents on it because they live in Italy and I live in Canada.

3 ....
   There *is / are* lots of videos on this site. My friends like the ones with the funny cats, but I prefer watching music videos.

4 ....
   My mother loves this site! You *can / can't* buy anything from it, but it's a good place to tell your friends what you are doing.

6 Complete the description of Wikipedia with the words in the box.
Use one word twice.

> are   can   is   this

Log in | Create account

There **(1)** .... lots of information on Wikipedia about lots of different subjects. For example, you **(2)** .... find out about Hollywood stars, the history of the word 'OK' or the life of the great scientist Marie Curie. There **(3)** .... millions of articles in lots of languages on **(4)** .... site and anyone can add more information to them. **(5)** .... website is for people who really enjoy finding things out.

WIKIPEDIA
The Free Encyclopedia

7 Write about the social networking website Twitter. Use *there is / there are*, *you can*, *this* and this information:

What is it?	social networking (or 'microblogging') website
What can you do on it?	post short messages (140 letters or fewer)
Why is it useful?	find out what is happening very quickly
Why do people like it?	fun and easy to use

....
....
....
....
....
....
....
....

11 City living
It's a great place for tourists

VOCABULARY

1 Complete the sentences with the words in the box. Use the plural form if necessary.

> bridge   cathedral   mosque   palace   ~~square~~   stadium   statue   temple

0 Zócalo in Mexico City is one of the biggest ....*squares*.... in the world.

1 Prague, the capital of the Czech Republic, has lots of ....

2 One of the most beautiful .... in Spain is in Santiago de Compostela.

3 You can see Michaelangelo's .... of David in Florence in Italy.

4 The Sultan Ahmed .... is in Istanbul.

5 You can visit the Winter .... in St Petersburg.

6 The Maracanã is a famous football .... in Rio.

7 Ankgor Wat is a .... in Cambodia.

2 Match the descriptions to the places.

1 This is where people teach and study different subjects. There is a famous one in Harvard, USA.
2 You go here to eat a meal.
3 If you would you like to do some exercise, this is the place for you.
4 This is a building with a collection of books that you can borrow.
5 If you want to tell a police officer about a problem, you go here.
6 You go here to catch a train.
7 When you're ill, you need to go here.
8 You go here to buy stamps.
9 You go here to walk and have a picnic.
10 You go here to look around and to buy things.

a sports centre
b police station
c train station
d post office
e library
f university
g shop
h hospital
i park
j restaurant

GRAMMAR Determiners

3 Choose the right words to complete the descriptions of cities.

1 This is one of *a / the* most beautiful cities in Europe. It's *a / the* capital of the Netherlands and it's famous for its bridges and museums. It's *a / the* great place for riding a bike.

2 This is one of *a / the* biggest cities in the United States of America. Tourists come here to see the Statue of Liberty and visit the Museum of Modern Art. The city is known as *all / both* 'the city that never sleeps' and 'the Big Apple.'

3 This city is in the United Kingdom. There are many reasons to visit this city – the parks, museums and shops are *all / both* excellent. *Another / Other* reason visitors come here is to go to the theatre. The Olympic Games were here in 2012.

4 This city is the capital of Russia. *A / The* square in its centre is one of the most famous in the world. There is a beautiful cathedral here, as well as lots of *other / another* interesting buildings.

4 Read the descriptions again. What are the cities?

1 ....
2 ....
3 ....
4 ....

5 ⊙ Students often make mistakes with determiners. Correct the mistakes in three of these sentences. Which two sentences are correct?

1 I live on the Black Street at Number 10.

....

2 Vancouver has both mountains and beaches.

....

3 All the students were waiting to go into the new museum.

....
....

4 We had an sports competition today.

....

5 I want a penfriend in other country.

....

WRITING

6 Complete the article with the words in the box. Use some words more than once.

> a   all   both   the

CARDIFF

Cardiff is in Wales. It's **(1)** .... capital city. It's **(2)** .... small city, but it's **(3)** .... biggest one in Wales. Cardiff is near the sea and it's a friendly place. It's **(4)** .... good city to visit because there is a lot to do there. It has parks, shops and restaurants. It has **(5)** .... theatres and stadiums. **(6)** .... the road signs in Cardiff are in two languages: Welsh and English. **(7)** .... languages are spoken in Cardiff, but the first language of most of the people is English.

7 Now write about the capital city of your country. Use *a/an, the, both, all, other* and *another* in your description.

....
....
....
....
....
....
....
....
....
....

Do you mind if I sit here?

VOCABULARY

1 Replace the <u>underlined</u> parts of the sentences with words and phrases in the box.

> animals   children   details   luggage   ~~shop assistants~~
> the right size   you can get it   visit the website

Our <u>staff</u> will help you if you have any questions.

0 ...shop assistants...

<u>Information</u> can be found on our website.

4 ....

 Please leave your <u>suitcases</u> at the reception desk.

1 ....

<u>Under 16s</u> do not have to pay anything to enter.

5 ....

 <u>Dogs</u> are not allowed in the shop.

2 ....

If you want more information about the history of the museum, <u>it is available</u> here.

6 ....

<u>Go online</u> for more information about our products.

3 ....

If you can't find <u>a bigger or a smaller pair</u>, ask a member of staff.

7 ....

GRAMMAR   Uncountable nouns

2 Complete the table with the words in the box.

> advice   apartment   book   car
> electricity   food   hobby   homework
> luggage   money   physics   restaurant
> river   visitor

Countable	Uncountable
....	....
....	....
....	....
....	....
....	....
....	....
....	....

3 Complete the sentences with the words in the box.

> a lot of   bottles   many
> much   piece   slices

1 How .... video games have you got?
2 Would you like a .... of chocolate cake?
3 We've got some orange juice, some lemonade and three .... of water.
4 Can I have six .... of ham, please? No, that's too many, sorry. Only five, please.
5 Daniel's got .... old coins. His hobby is collecting them.
6 We haven't got .... homework to do this weekend.

LISTENING

4 ▶12 **Listen to the message from the New Theatre and choose the right words.**

January at the New Theatre

January 11 – January 13
(1) *Money / Honey* Talks are playing songs from their number one album. Tickets are cheaper if you buy them **(2)** *on the internet / at the theatre*.

January 14 – January 16
Professor Clinton Richards is talking about his new book *I Know Everything*. The first **(3)** *five / thirty-five* people to

buy a ticket will meet Professor Richards in the theatre **(4)** *restaurant / café*.

January 18 – January 24
A new play called *The End* is on at **(5)** *7.00 / 7.30* on Monday, Tuesday, Wednesday and Thursday and **(6)** *7.45 / 8.00* on Friday and Saturday.

READING

EXAM TIPS

Reading Part 1
- Always think about the topic of the different texts.
- Look for words in notices (A–H) that match what each sentence is saying.

5 ⬤ **Which notice (A–H) says this (1–5)? For questions 1–5, choose the correct letter (A–H).**

Example:

0	You can't buy tickets after this time.	C
1	If you are ten or younger, you do not have to pay for a ticket.	☐
2	Do not use your camera in this building.	☐
3	You must not eat your own food here.	☐
4	You can ask these people for information.	☐
5	Go online for extra details.	☐

A
Museum guides will answer visitors' questions about artists and paintings.

B

No picnics in this area

C
Last tickets sold at 5.00 pm

D
Free tours of the museum with top artists on Saturdays.
No more than 10 in group.

E

Use the internet and enjoy fresh sandwiches at the Museum Café (open until 4.00 pm).

F
Children under 11 can enter museum for free

G

NO PHOTOGRAPHS INSIDE THE MUSEUM

H
See our website for more information (including photos)

12 Festivals and films
It's a festival that everyone loves

VOCABULARY

1 Look at the pictures and write the words.

| drum | guitar | keyboard | trumpet | violin |

1 .... 2 ....

3 .... 4 ....

5 ....

2 Complete the words to make types of music.

1 b l .... s
2 c l .... s s .... c l
3 j .... z ....
4 f .... l ....
5 r ....
6 p ....
7 r .... k
8 s l

GRAMMAR   Relative pronouns *who*, *which*, *that*

3 Circle the right words to complete the email.

Hi Martha
Do you want to see No Direction? They're
playing in the Rose Bowl next week.
Everyone **(1)** *who / which* sees them in
concert says they're brilliant.
At the concert there'll also be a singer
(2) *who / which* comes from my town! Her
name's Meryl Dole and she's great. She
played at the Fun in the Sun festival **(3)** *who /
which* happens every July. She plays music
(4) *who / that* is a bit different. You'll see!
Anyway, let me know if you want to come.
We need to get tickets soon!
Love
Eddie

4 Change *that* in the advertisement to *who* or *which*.

Fun in the Sun Festival

Come to the Fun in the Sun Festival. It's a
place for singers **(0)** *that* are unusual. The
festival is in a beautiful house **(1)** *that* has
a really big garden. Great for a summer
picnic! There's even a lake **(2)** *that* you can
swim in. Everyone **(3)** *that* comes to our
festival really enjoys it. It's friendly and fun,
but it's not free! Tickets are £99 for three
days. For people **(4)** *that* are under 16 the
tickets cost £79 for three days. What are
you waiting for? Buy your tickets now!

0 ....who..........
1 ....
2 ....
3 ....
4 ....

5 🔘 **Students often make mistakes with relative pronouns. Which sentence is right (✔)?**

1 a Yesterday I bought a black jacket and a pair of jeans who are blue. ....

 b Yesterday I bought a black jacket and a pair of jeans which are blue. ....

2 a When you come here we can go swimming in the lake who is near my house. ....

 b When you come here we can go swimming in the lake that is near my house. ....

3 a Last Saturday I bought a white skirt which cost forty dollars. ....

 b Last Saturday I bought a white skirt wich cost forty dollars. ....

4 a My favourite birthday present is my bike. It was Jim gave it to me. ....

 b My favourite birthday present is my bike. It was Jim who gave it to me. ....

5 a You need to bring three pencils and the book that the teacher will give you. ....

 b You need to bring three pencils and the book who the teacher will give you. ....

WRITING

EXAM TIPS

Writing Part 8
- Always read the information in the text(s) very carefully.
- Check that you have copied everything correctly including any numbers.

6 🔘 **Read the advertisement and the email to Aaron. Fill in the information in Aaron's notes.**

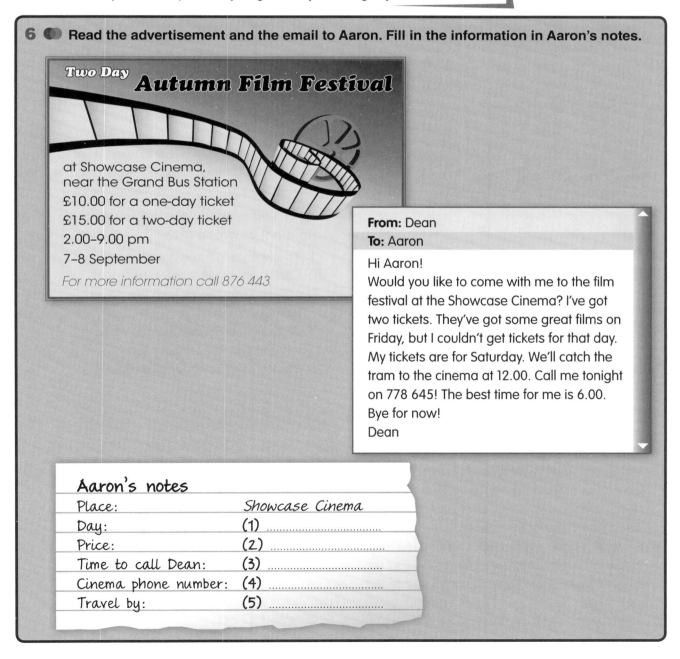

Two Day **Autumn Film Festival**

at Showcase Cinema,
near the Grand Bus Station
£10.00 for a one-day ticket
£15.00 for a two-day ticket
2.00–9.00 pm
7–8 September

For more information call 876 443

From: Dean
To: Aaron

Hi Aaron!
Would you like to come with me to the film festival at the Showcase Cinema? I've got two tickets. They've got some great films on Friday, but I couldn't get tickets for that day. My tickets are for Saturday. We'll catch the tram to the cinema at 12.00. Call me tonight on 778 645! The best time for me is 6.00.
Bye for now!
Dean

Aaron's notes		
Place:		Showcase Cinema
Day:	(1)	....
Price:	(2)	....
Time to call Dean:	(3)	....
Cinema phone number:	(4)	....
Travel by:	(5)	....

This film looks exciting!

READING

1 Read the email and answer the questions.

> Hi Danuta
>
> What are you doing on Saturday afternoon? Would you like to come to the theatre? Ayla and I are going to see a new musical called *Monkey Around*. Actually, I really wanted to see *High School Superstar* at the cinema instead, but Ayla doesn't want to watch it. Do you know the Lux Theatre? It only opened last year. It's the one opposite the bus station. The other one, The Royal, is closed at the moment.
>
> The show is on twice on Saturday, first at 3.00 and then at 7.30. We're going to see it in the afternoon. 7.30 is too late for us. We're meeting at the train station on Turing Place at 1.00. The theatre is only a ten-minute walk from there. I hope you can come.
>
> Love
> Pablo

1 What did Pablo want to do?

....

2 Where is the Lux Theatre?

....

3 What time are they going to see *Monkey Around*?

....

4 How are they getting to the theatre?

....

GRAMMAR Conjunctions

2 Choose the right word to complete the sentences.

1 Would you like to go to the cinema *when / while* you finish your homework, Lucas?

2 There is a cinema in my town *if / where* they give you a piece cake for free during the film.

3 I enjoy listening to classical music *where / while* I'm doing my homework.

4 *While / If* I finish my project, I'll come to the theatre with you. But don't wait for me. I'm not sure I'll be able to finish my project before the play starts.

5 Pablo says *if / that* the musical is on twice on Saturdays.

3 Now match the sentences in Exercise 2 to the replies.

a Really? That sounds great. I hope it's a chocolate one. ....

b Yes, I would! There's a new film I'd really like to see. ....

c OK. Let me know. ....

d Me too! I really like Bach and Mozart. ....

e What time does it start? ....

LISTENING

4 ▶13 Listen to Marina talking to Chris about a film festival and choose the right answer (a or b).

1 Chris can't go to the film festival on ....
   a Thursday   b Saturday

2 Chris is going to a party on ....
   a Thursday   b Friday

3 Chris thinks *Mouse Man* might be ....
   a funny   b stupid

4 Marina .... watch *Mouse Man*.
   a wants to   b doesn't want to

5 Chris and Marina decide to watch ....
   a *Boston*   b *Mouse Man*

5 ▶13 Listen again. Are the sentences right (✔) or wrong (✗)?

1 The festival is three days long. ....

2 Chris's cousin is thirteen now. ....

3 *Mouse Man* and *Boston* are on at different times. ....

4 Chris thinks *Boston* sounds more interesting than *Mouse Man*. ....

5 *Mouse Man* is longer than *Boston*. ....

Prepare to write an invitation

6 Complete the advertisements with *on*, *at* and *to*. Then match the advertisements to the pictures.

1 THE **CIRCUS** IS IN TOWN!

Come **(1)** .... the All New Scotland State Circus **(2)** .... 18 Salmond Gardens, Edinburgh.
See the Amazing Flying McDougal fly through the air and watch Tartan Tom as he eats fire! Yes, that's right! Tartan Tom can eat fire.
The All New Scotland State Circus is better than ever before! We've got lots of new things for you to enjoy.
All the fun starts **(3)** .... Saturday the 18th of July
(4) .... 7.00! The last show is **(5)** .... Wednesday the 22nd of July.

2 THE DOOR TO **ANOTHER** WORLD!

(6) .... the Sir Anthony Hopkins Theatre
(7) .... Hannibal Street **(8)** .... Friday evening **(9)** .... 7.00, we've got a new play by a young writer from Poland called Tomas Zlin.
The Portal is about four teenagers who find a door to another world in the middle of their school.

3 ★★★ THE FILM OF THE YEAR ★★★

(10) .... Friday evening **(11)** .... 8.00, there is only one place to be: The Universe Cinema, **(12)** .... Hitchcock Street.
Watch Michael Farrell and Jennifer Roberts in a great new film called *The Invitation*. It's the story of how one text message changes everyone's lives.
Come **(13)** .... the Universe and find out how!

a

b

Text Message:

The Universe, this Friday. Don't be late.

reply   save   delete

c

7 Now write an email inviting your friend to an event. Include this information:

1 the type of event (e.g. concert, play, musical, circus, show, film)
2 the name of the place
3 the time the event starts
4 who is going to watch it
5 how you are getting there

....
....
....
....
....
....
....
....
....

13 Life experiences
Have you ever wanted to be a chef?

VOCABULARY

1 Find ten jobs.

r	e	c	e	p	t	i	o	n	i	s	t
h	d	e	n	t	i	s	t	l	n	p	o
c	o	l	m	j	w	r	r	x	b	v	u
p	h	o	t	o	g	r	a	p	h	e	r
b	c	e	r	n	d	a	b	w	t	l	g
n	m	o	f	h	r	e	r	k	l	h	u
o	p	i	l	o	t	r	l	t	n	k	i
r	w	e	n	k	d	m	n	b	i	e	d
l	n	u	r	s	e	x	t	e	r	s	e
m	e	c	h	a	n	i	c	n	e	j	t

2 Complete the sentences with the words from Exercise 1.
Use the plural form if necessary.

1 The .... on our trip was great. She told us lots of stories
about Dublin.

2 Being a .... is not an easy job. They often work many hours
looking after people in hospital.

3 My cousin is a .... at a restaurant in London.

4 The .... at the hotel was very kind to us when we had
a problem with our room.

5 Velazquez, Rembrandt and Michelangelo are three of the most famous
.... in history.

6 Amelia Earhart was one of the most well-known .... of the
twentieth century. She was the first woman to fly alone across the Atlantic.

7 My father is a .... I think teeth are boring, but he thinks
they are very interesting.

8 I'd like to be a .... My parents gave me a camera for my
birthday and I take photos with it every day.

9 My uncle is a .... I often see his face in magazines.

10 My sister is a .... She loves cars and she's very good
at repairing them.

GRAMMAR Present perfect with *ever* and *never*

3 **Write complete questions. Use the present perfect.**

0 talk / famous person
Have you ever talked to a famous person ?

1 live / another country
.... ?

2 listen / Johann Sebastian Bach
.... ?

3 play / trumpet
.... ?

4 cook / Indian food
.... ?

5 climb / mountain
.... ?

4 **Now write your answers to the questions in Exercise 3. Use *Yes, I have.* and *No, I haven't.***

0 ...No, I haven't. ....

1 ....

2 ....

3 ....

4 ....

5 ....

5 **Complete the sentences with the correct form of the verbs in the box.**

listen   live   play   visit   work

1 I've never .... to jazz.

2 My sister has never .... in a shop.

3 Richard has never .... in an apartment in Spain.

4 My parents have never .... Naples in Italy.

5 Emily has never .... a musical instrument.

6 ⊙ **Students often make mistakes with the present perfect with *ever* and *never*. Correct the mistakes in three of these sentences. Which two sentences are correct?**

1 I've never joined a sports club.
....

2 I have to tell you that this have never happened before.
....
....

3 Have you ever cooked a meal for your family?
....

4 Ayrton Senna was the best Formula 1 driver that have ever lived.
....
....

5 I really like *Call of Juarez*. It's the best video game that I have never played.
....
....

READING

EXAM TIPS

Reading Part 2
- When answering multiple-choice questions, always try each option before you decide which one is right.
- Look at the words before and after the spaces.

7 ⬤ **Read the sentences about Louise's job. Choose the best word (A, B or C) for each space.**

Example:

0 Louise .... her new job last week.
Ⓐ started   **B** opened   **C** arrived

1 Louise works for an international music .... in London.
A factory   **B** market   **C** company

2 Louise's office is in the .... of the city.
A centre   **B** square   **C** street

3 Louise is very .... about her work.
A lucky   **B** excited   **C** special

4 Louise .... to a famous singer yesterday.
A told   **B** said   **C** spoke

5 Louise really .... her first week at work.
A spent   **B** enjoyed   **C** made

No, I've never done that

VOCABULARY

1 Write complete questions. Use the present perfect + *ever*.

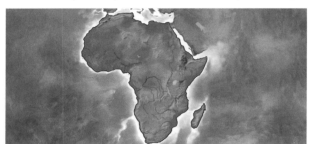

0 be / Africa

....Have you ever been to Africa............ ?

1 eat / Mexican food

.... ?

2 break / arm or leg

.... ?

3 meet / footballer

.... ?

4 ride / motorbike

.... ?

5 wear / unusual clothes

.... ?

2 Now match the questions in Exercise 2 to the answers.

a Yes, I have. I met some of the
Real Madrid players after a match. ....

b No, I haven't, but I'd really like to
go there. ....0....

c No, I haven't. I'm not interested in
how I look. ....

d Yes, I have. I went to Cancun with my
parents last year and we ate it there. ....

e No, I haven't, but I'd like to travel
around the USA on one. ....

f No, I haven't. But I broke a toe when
I was five years old. ....

3 Write questions with *Have you ever ...*
and the verbs.

1 ....
(be)?

2 ....
(meet)?

3 ....
(eat)?

4 ....
(wear)?

5 ....
(ride)?

6 ....
(break)?

LISTENING

4 ▶14 **Listen to Rick Thomas's interview with Christine Wilson. Which experiences has Christine had (✔)?**

0 eaten Chinese food ....✔....

1 been to Brazil ....

2 climbed a mountain ....

3 played the piano ....

4 broken her arm ....

5 worked in a restaurant ....

5 ▶14 **Listen to the interview again. Who says what? Write *R* for Rick and *C* for Christine.**

1 I think it would be a lot of fun. ....

2 I went last summer. ....

3 My brother is a very good climber. ....

4 What about you? ....

5 Did you enjoy it? ....

READING

6 **Complete the conversation with the words in the box.**

> ever   have   haven't   never

Rob: Hi, Anna.

Anna: Hi, Rob. What are you reading?

Rob: Oh, it's a questionnaire. There are lots of them on this website. Have you **(1)** .... looked at the site? It's called experience.co.uk.

Anna: No, I've **(2)** .... seen it before. What are the questions?

Rob: I'll read you some.

Anna: Great.

Rob: OK. Have you ever grown your own vegetables?

Anna: No, I haven't. But my parents grow lots of different things.

Rob: Have you ever fallen asleep in the cinema?

Anna: Yes, I **(3)** .... ! I fell asleep last week during that terrible film about the students who want to be singers.

Rob: Have you ever dreamed you were famous?

Anna: No, I **(4)** .... I don't want to be famous, Rob!

Rob: Next question: have you ever forgotten to do your homework?

Anna: Lots of times. Don't look at me like that, Rob.

Rob: Well, I always do *my* homework.

Anna: No, you don't. Last week you wanted to look at my maths homework.

Rob: Almost always, then.

7 **Read the conversation again. Are the sentences right (✔) or wrong (✗)?**

1 Anna doesn't know the website. ....

2 Anna grows her own vegetables. ....

3 Anna didn't enjoy the film she saw last week. ....

4 Anna wants to be famous. ....

5 Rob always does his homework. ....

14 Spending money
It's just opened

VOCABULARY

1 Look at the pictures and write the words.

> bookshop   café   chemist   clothes shop   department store
> market   shoe shop   supermarket   sweet shop

1 ....

2 ....

3 ....

4 ....

5 ....

6 ....

7 ....

8 ....

9 ....

2 Find the odd one out. Which things can't you buy in these places?

0 bookshop	dictionary	notebook	(drum)	diary
1 café	coffee	cake	sandwich	video game
2 clothes shop	jacket	map	trousers	T-shirt
3 market	bananas	carrots	bus ticket	eggs
4 shoe shop	shoes	trainers	boots	football
5 supermarket	piano	newspaper	meat	bread
6 sweet shop	chocolate	tomatoes	lemonade	sweets

GRAMMAR   Present perfect with *just, yet* and *already*

3 Choose the right words to complete the sentences.

1 Have you been to the new clothes shop *yet* / *just*?

2 Susan has *just* / *already* missed the train. It left two minutes ago.

3 The new supermarket has *already* / *yet* opened. I went there last week.

4 I've *just* / *yet* seen Jon. He was in his favourite place: the sweet shop.

5 I haven't been to the market *yet* / *already*. Do you need anything?

6 I've *already* / *just* seen that film three times. I love it!

4 Complete the conversation with *yet* and *already.*

Nicola: What's wrong?

Alex: I haven't finished my history project
(1) ....

Nicola: That's OK. We don't have to give it to Mr Cameron until Monday.

Alex: Have you finished yours?

Nicola: Yes, I've **(2)** .... done mine.

Alex: I'm too busy, Nicola. I've got too many projects to do.

Nicola: Have you done your geography project **(3)** .... ?

Alex: Yes, I have. I did that this morning.

Nicola: Have you had a break **(4)** .... ?

Alex: Yes, I've **(5)** .... had a five-minute break today.

Nicola: That's not enough!

Alex: But there's so much history to read, Nicola. Mr Cameron won't be happy if I don't finish this.

5 What's just happened? Write complete sentences.

0 Paul / eat / sandwich
Paul has just eaten a sandwich.

1 Mary / play / tennis match
....
....

2 Adam / get home
....
....

3 Joseph and Peter / see / concert
....
....

4 Eve and Julia / leave / shoe shop
....
....

6 👁 Students often make mistakes with the present perfect with *just, yet, already.* Correct the mistakes in three of these sentences. Which two sentences are correct?

1 I'm in England. I have not seen nothing yet because it's rained every day.
....
....

2 I'm going to paint my bedroom next week, and you've already said that you're going to help me.
....
....

3 I've just had a birthday and my friend Jane bought me a CD.
....
....

4 Yesterday, I left a book at your house and I need it because I don't do my homework yet.
....
....

5 I'm just watched the football game with my family. It was really fun.
....
....

READING

7 Choose the right words (a or b) to complete the article.

HOW TO STOP SPENDING MONEY

Do you **(1)** .... too much money? Lots of teenagers love shopping, but do you go to department stores every weekend and **(2)** .... too many expensive things? Read on for our advice.

- **(3)** .... a list of what you spend your money on. Look at it at the end of the month. You'll probably be surprised.
- Ask yourself: why am I buying this object? Do I **(4)** .... it or do I only **(5)** .... it at this moment?
- **(6)** .... things that are fun and free: talk to friends, go for a walk, ride your bike, borrow a book from the library.

1	**a** buy	**b** spend
2	**a** save	**b** buy
3	**a** Make	**b** Do
4	**a** need	**b** know
5	**a** want	**b** get
6	**a** Have	**b** Do

Let's have three slices each

VOCABULARY

1 **Match the letters and symbols to the words.**

1	cm	a	cents
2	kg	b	litres
3	€	c	pence
4	c	d	euros
5	ml	e	grams
6	m	f	millilitres
7	£	g	kilometres
8	p	h	centimetres
9	l	i	kilograms
10	g	j	pounds
11	km	k	metres

2 **Complete the text with the words in the box.**

> bit   pair   set   slices   variety

It was my birthday yesterday and I bought myself some presents. I spent all of my birthday money! I bought a (1) .... of trainers, some pens in a (2) .... of different colours and a (3) .... of Robert Pattinson DVDs. At lunchtime I had two (4) .... of carrot cake, some biscuits and a (5) .... of chocolate.

LISTENING

3 ▶15 **Listen to Harry talking to Marie about a shopping trip. Match the people to the objects they bought.**

1	Eddie	**a**	a video game
2	Paul	**b**	a pair of sunglasses
3	Lauren	**c**	a coat
4	Ingrid	**d**	a book about films
5	Harry	**e**	a pair of shoes

4 ▶15 **Listen again. Are the sentences right (✔) or wrong (✗)?**

1 Marie went on a shopping trip
with Harry.   ....

2 Eddie bought a jacket.   ....

3 Lauren bought a book.   ....

4 Ingrid saw a jacket that she liked. ....

5 Harry likes the thing he bought.   ....

Prepare to write a note

5 **Add capital letters, apostrophes, full stops and question marks to the sentences.**

               Nicola
0 I've just seen ~~nicola~~.

1 What time shall we meet

2 Lets go home.

3 I need to buy something from the market

4 I saw mr Smith yesterday.

6 **Write the notes with capital letters, apostrophes, full stops and question marks.**

1

dear Vicky
i cant wait to see the film it
sounds really good shall we meet
at the cinema at 6
see you soon
ivan
....
....
....
....

2

hi paula
were going to the new shopping centre
tomorrow do you want to come with us
love
stefano
....
....
....

WRITING

EXAM TIPS

Writing Part 9

- Always check your grammar, spelling and punctuation.
- Use informal English because you are writing to a friend.

7 ● **You are going to meet your friend Naomi in town on Saturday. Write a note to Naomi.**
Say:
what time you will meet
where you will meet
which shops you want to go to
Write 25–35 words.

....
....
....
....
....
....
....

15 Free time
I've had a guitar since I was ten

VOCABULARY

1 Read about people's hobbies. Write the activities with the people.

acting   chatting   collecting   cooking   doing   going
listening   making   playing   reading   spending   watching

Jack

What do I like doing in my free time?
(1) .... !
I do it as often as I can. There are four books next to my bed at the moment.

Mathew

(7) ....
out with friends and doing sport. The perfect Saturday? A game of football and then a trip to the cinema.

Tanya

My favourite hobby is
(2) ....
things. I use all sorts of things: plastic, wood, paper. I'd like to be an artist in the future.

Pilar

Oh, I do lots of different things. I like playing computer games and
(8) ....
TV. I like
(9) .... to music too.

Diana

My hobby? That's easy:
(3) ....
photography! I never leave the house without my camera.

Altan

In my free time I love
(10) ....
musical instruments. At the moment I'm learning the guitar, drums and trumpet.

Guillermo

(4) .... is my favourite thing to do when I'm not in school. I usually prepare Italian food, but I also like making dishes from other countries.

Lev

Three things: singing,
(11) ....
and dancing. I go to a theatre group every Saturday. I love it!

Galina

I really like
(5) ....
time on my computer and
(6) .... to other people online. I live on the internet!

Natalie

I enjoy
(12) ....
things that we usually don't keep: train tickets, receipts, newspapers.

GRAMMAR Present perfect with *since/for*

2 Choose the right word to complete the sentences.

1 I've had my phone *for / since* six months.
2 She's had her computer *for / since* 2013.
3 They've lived there *for / since* last summer.
4 He's only played the guitar *for / since* three weeks.
5 I haven't seen my cousins *for / since* a long time.
6 We have known each other *for / since* we were ten years old.

3 Match the questions to the answers.

1 How long have you lived in your house? ....
2 How long has he collected badges? ....
3 How long have you played the piano? ....
4 How long has she played basketball? ....
5 How long has he known his best friend? ....
6 How long has she had her camera? ....

a Since I was five years old. It's my favourite instrument!
b For ten years. They lived in the same street when they were little boys.
c Since last month. She loves it! She takes lots of photos.
d Only for a week. I miss our old place.
e Since he was ten years old. He's got lots of them!
f For four years. She catches and throws the ball very well.

4 ⊙ Students often make mistakes with the present perfect with *for* and *since*. Which sentence is right (✔)?

1 a It's so nice that you'll come tomorrow. I didn't see you for three weeks. ....
  b It's so nice that you'll come tomorrow. I haven't seen you for three weeks. ....
2 a I didn't eat chicken since a long time. ....
  b I haven't eaten chicken for a long time. ....
3 a Yesterday I bought two dresses. I haven't had one since I was six! ....
  b Yesterday I bought two dresses. I've never had one since I was six! ....
4 a I want to sell my radio. I've had it for four years. ....
  b I want to sell my radio. I've got it since four years. ....
5 a I know Adam twenty years. ....
  b I've known Adam for twenty years. ....

READING

5 Choose the right words (a or b) to complete the blog.

My friends spend **(1)** .... their free time chatting online. They sit in front **(2)** .... their computers **(3)** .... hours. But I don't like chatting online. I prefer collecting postcards. 'Why do you do it, Paula?' my friends ask me. They don't know why I do it, but that is OK.
I've collected postcards **(4)** .... I was six years old. I'm thirteen now. I started when my uncle sent me a postcard **(5)** .... Madrid. The next one was from my cousin who went on holiday to Milan. After that, I asked my friends and family to send me postcards when they went somewhere new.
When I first started getting postcards, I put them on the walls of my bedroom. Then I put them on the ceiling. Then I started putting them **(6)** .... boxes. I've filled fifty boxes and have 5,213 postcards from almost **(7)** .... country in the world!

1 a all   b every
2 a from   b of
3 a since   b for
4 a since   b for
5 a from   b since
6 a of   b in
7 a all   b every

6 Read the blog again and choose the right answer (a or b).

1 Paula .... chatting online.
  a enjoys   b doesn't enjoy
2 Paula's friends .... why she collects postcards.
  a understand   b don't understand
3 Paula has collected postcards for ....
  a six years   b seven years
4 Paula's first postcard was from ....
  a Spain   b Italy
5 Paula put her first postcards ....
  a on the walls   b in boxes

Birthday challenges

VOCABULARY

1 Find six verbs.

c	b	t	i	d	v
l	p	o	q	x	o
e	k	a	o	h	r
a	o	g	y	k	d
n	l	r	e	z	e
r	e	p	a	i	r

2 Write the verbs from Exercise 1 with the pictures.

1 .... a 15-km run

2 .... the car

3 .... a hotel

4 .... a shelf

5 .... a pizza

6 .... a bill

3 Now complete the sentences with the phrases from Exercise 2.
Use the plural form and change the form of the verb if necessary.

1 My parents .... online, but my grandparents still
do this at the post office.

2 There's nothing in the fridge, so let's .... for dinner
this evening.

3 Thank you for .... , Jane. It looks great!

4 Before we went to Liverpool last month, we ....
on the internet.

5 My brother's very fit! He .... last week.

6 Do you know how to .... ? The one in my bedroom
was broken, but I watched an online video and learned how to fix it.

LISTENING

4 ▶16 **Listen to the conversation between Charlie and Dan and choose the right answer (a or b).**

1 It's .... birthday.
   a Charlie's   **b** Dan's

2 Dan's .... is in Italy.
   a mum   **b** dad

3 Dan .... the video game.
   a knows   **b** doesn't know

4 .... has bought a cake.
   a Dan   **b** Charlie

5 ▶16 **Listen again. Which things has Dan done (✔)?**

1 repaired something   ....
2 cut something   ....
3 cleaned something   ....
4 made someone some food   ....
5 bought something   ....
6 played something   ....
7 tidied something   ....
8 washed something   ....

WRITING

EXAM TIPS

Writing Part 9
- Use adjectives and adverbs to make your writing more interesting.
- Make notes about each question before you begin writing.

6 💿 **Read the email from your English friend Stefanie.**

From:	Stefanie
To:	

Hi
Sorry I couldn't come to your party on Saturday. Who was there? What did your parents get you for your birthday? What was your favourite present?
Love
Stefanie

7 Write Stefanie an email. Answer the questions.
   Write 25–35 words.

16 So many languages!
He has learned 11 languages

GRAMMAR Present perfect and past simple

1 Choose the right word (a or b) to complete the questions.

1 .... you ever studied Arabic?
   a Have   **b** Did

2 Did you .... any tests in school last week?
   a do   **b** done

3 .... anyone in your family learned to speak another language?
   a Have   **b** Has

4 When .... you first study English?
   a do   **b** did

5 How many films have you .... in English?
   a watched   **b** watch

2 Now write your answers to the questions in Exercise 1.

1 ....
2 ....
3 ....
4 ....
5 ....

3 Write sentences in the present perfect or past simple.

0 she / work / in New Zealand and South Africa
   ...She's worked in New Zealand and...
   ...South Africa.

1 I / never / meet / someone / from the USA
   ....

2 we / go / on holiday / last year
   ....

3 he / study / Chinese and Arabic
   ....

4 they / not / travel / by plane
   ....

5 she / watch / great cricket match / on Saturday
   ....

6 he / win / lots of chess competitions
   ....

7 we / see / my grandparents / two weeks ago
   ....

8 I / never / eat / Mexican food
   ....

4 Complete the sentences with the present perfect or past simple form of the verbs in the box.

not go   not study   play   read   see   speak

1 .... you ever .... a 500-page book?

2 I .... Russian at school last year. I chose to do German instead.

3 We .... on holiday last summer. We stayed at home.

4 My brother .... never .... a musical instrument.

5 .... you .... to Charlie about the party yet?

6 .... you .... Joseph yesterday?

5 ⊙ Students often make mistakes with the present perfect and the past simple. <u>Underline</u> six mistakes in the email.

Hi David
It's been ages since I haven't heard from you! I'm in London now. I'm studying at the Camden School of English! I've met lots of people from all over the world. The teacher is good and the textbook she gave us is very interesting. I learn a lot of things from it. Every day, after class, we go into the centre of London. I've already done lots of things! I've the British Museum. It was great!
I've went shopping yesterday and bought some clothes. I've bought three T-shirts because they were very cheap and they look really nice. They have only cost me £20.
Right, I must go now. I've got to study for an English test tomorrow – it's on the present perfect.
Love
Danuta

6 Now correct the mistakes.

1 ....
2 ....
3 ....
4 ....
5 ....
6 ....

VOCABULARY

7 Complete the text with the words in the box. Use the plural form if necessary.

> article   chat   dictionary   exercise   guess
> interesting   list   mistake   spell

IDEAS FOR **LEARNING LANGUAGES**

Home | About us | Contact us

We'd like to give you some ideas for learning languages. Learning languages is one of the most **(1)** .... things you can do with your free time. It's hard work, but it's also a lot of fun. These are some things you can do to help improve your level in the languages you are studying.

- Do grammar **(2)** .... Grammar is very important.
- **(3)** .... to lots of different people as often as you can.
- Read as much as you can – magazine **(4)** .... , books, websites.
- Don't worry about making **(5)** ....
- Learn how to **(6)** .... words correctly.
- Make a **(7)** .... of new vocabulary and then play games with the words to help you learn them.
- When you read or hear a word you don't know, try to **(8)** .... its meaning. You can then check in your **(9)** ....
- Listen as often as you can – to the radio, to songs, and to people talking.

LISTENING

EXAM TIPS

Listening Part 1
- Listen carefully to the recording both times it is played.
- Look at the pictures and think about the question before you listen.

8 ⬤ ▶17 **You will hear five short conversations. There is one question for each conversation. For each question, choose the right answer (A, B or C).**

Example:

0 What will the weather be like tomorrow?

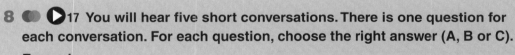

1 When is the history test?

3 What time will the football match finish?

2 Where is the girl's purse?

4 How much did Sally pay for her keyboard?

£50   £100   £450

5 What is the girl's father doing now?

Languages of the world

VOCABULARY

1 Look at the pictures and write the words.

> board   dictionary   library   magazine   message   textbook

1 ....

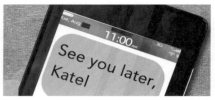

2 ....

3 ....

4 ....

5 ....

6 ....

2 Complete the sentences with the words from Exercise 1.

1 I got a strange text .... last night. It read 'hst soiqj wwww.' I don't know what it means!

2 The .... in our classroom is next to the door.

3 I really enjoy learning history, but I don't like the .... our teacher uses.

4 My brother uses websites to find the meanings of words, but I prefer to use my old ....

5 We have a great .... in our town. I usually borrow two books a week from it.

6 I read a .... for language learners every month. It's always full of interesting articles.

READING

3 Complete the conversation with the words in the box.

> does   grew   had   have   love   speaks   studied

Nick: Hi, David. **(1)** .... you had a class with our new Chinese teacher yet?

David: No, I haven't. Have you?

Nick: Yes, we **(2)** .... a class with her yesterday. Her name is Miss Lee. She's really good. She's from Hong Kong and she **(3)** .... five languages!

David: Really? Which ones?

Nick: Chinese, of course. And English, perfectly. She also knows Spanish, French and Russian.

David: **(4)** .... she have any family from Spain, France or Russia?

Nick: No, she doesn't. All her family are from China. She **(5)** .... up speaking Chinese at home and learned English in school.

David: What about the other languages?

Nick: Well, she **(6)** .... Spanish and French at university, and then she spent a few years living in Moscow. She learned Russian there.

David: I'd **(7)** .... to be able to speak five languages!

Nick: Me too!

4 Read the conversation again. Are the sentences right (✔) or wrong (✗)?

1 Miss Lee has taught Nick, but she hasn't taught David yet. ....

2 Miss Lee's English is excellent. ....

3 Miss Lee has family from Spain. ....

4 Miss Lee grew up speaking English at home. ....

5 Miss Lee learned Russian after studying at university. ....

Prepare to write information about your English class

5 Write the sentences with capital letters.

0 i really like studying languages in school. it's a lot of fun.

I really like studying languages in school. It's a lot of fun.

1 my friend boris is learning chinese.

2 i would like to learn russian, italian and turkish.

3 marta has lived in england for ten years, but she is spanish.

4 I want to live in another country when i'm older.

5 has dina passed her english exam?

6 brian is from ireland, but he lives in the usa.

6 Write the text with capital letters.

i'm studying english in a school near my house. my teacher's name is colin and he's from scotland. learning english is important because everyone speaks it. i like to learn english by reading, watching films and talking to people.

7 Now write a description of your English class. Remember to use capital letters. Include this information:

1 where you are studying English

2 your teacher's name and where he/she is from

3 the way you like to learn English

17 Staying healthy
I've hurt myself

VOCABULARY

1 **Put the letters in the right order to make words for parts of the body.**

1 y e e ....
2 e f a c ....
3 t o f o ....
4 n d h a ....
5 a e h d ....
6 t u o m h ....
7 s o n e ....
8 t o h o t ....

2 **Complete the sentences with words from Exercise 1. Use the plural form if necessary.**

1 I went to the dentist because one of my .... was hurting me.
2 What colour are your .... ?
3 When I was little girl, I had to hold my mum's .... when we crossed the road.
4 My grandmother always says 'don't eat with your .... open!'
5 I put my hat on because my .... was getting cold.
6 Look at my .... when you speak to me.

3 **Find nine parts of the body.**

s	t	o	m	a	c	h	b
j	u	o	l	g	t	e	l
w	v	c	e	i	b	a	o
e	y	n	j	e	a	r	o
b	r	a	i	n	c	t	d
r	j	n	e	c	k	e	s
d	z	k	x	c	b	m	l
b	f	f	i	n	g	e	r

GRAMMAR
Pronouns *myself, yourself, herself, himself, ourselves, yourselves, themselves*

4 **Complete the table.**

I	....	myself
you	you	....
he	....	....
she	....	
....	it	itself
we	us	....
you	....	....
they	them	....

5 **Choose the right word to complete the sentences.**

1 He made *herself / himself* a cup of tea.
2 I cut *themselves / myself* while I was making a pizza.
3 My sister lives by *herself / himself* in a flat in Venice.
4 They went to the basketball match by *myself / themselves.*
5 Grandma told us to help *myself / ourselves* to the cheese sandwiches.
6 I emailed *myself / herself* a link to the website.

6 **Complete the sentences.**

1 My mum always says 'take care of ....' when I leave the house.
2 She hurt .... when she fell off her bike.
3 'Help .... to chocolate cake,' my aunt told us when we got to her house.
4 He made the pizza by ....
5 We really enjoyed .... at Dan's birthday party.
6 I like to go to the cinema by ....

7 **Write the plural form of the sentences.**

0 He's teaching himself to speak Arabic.
......They're.teaching.themselves.to......
......speak.Arabic.......

1 Did you paint that wall by yourself?

....

2 I really enjoyed myself on holiday.

....

3 He bought himself a new video game.

....

4 She made the cake by herself.

....

5 I hurt myself playing football.

....

8 👁 **Students often make mistakes with pronouns. Correct the mistakes in three of these sentences. Which two sentences are correct?**

1 He hurt himself playing cricket.

....

2 Yesterday I went to buy me some clothes.

....

3 I'm so happy that I'm coming to your house tomorrow. We'll enjoy us.

....

4 You take care of your self.

....

5 She bought herself a new laptop.

....

9 🔘 **Read the article about the Brownlee brothers. Choose the best word (A, B, or C) for each space.**

Example:

0 **A** a   Ⓑ the   **C** one
1 **A** run   **B** running   **C** ran
2 **A** good   **B** better   **C** best
3 **A** by   **B** from   **C** with
4 **A** Them   **B** Theirs   **C** They
5 **A** already   **B** still   **C** yet
6 **A** at   **B** on   **C** by
7 **A** these   **B** those   **C** that
8 **A** or   **B** because   **C** but

READING

EXAM TIPS

Reading Part 5
- The second time you read something you will see things you didn't see the first time. Don't forget to read the text more than once!
- Look at the picture and think about the topic before you read the text.

The Brownlee brothers

Triathlon is one of the hardest sports in **(0)** .... world. Triathletes swim for 1.5 kilometres, cycle for 40 kilometres, and **(1)** .... for 10 kilometres. Two of the **(2)** .... triathletes are Alistair and Jonny Brownlee. The two brothers are **(3)** .... Yorkshire in the north of England. **(4)** .... practise every day. Both of them have **(5)** .... been world champions. Alistair is two years older than Jonny. He won the gold medal **(6)** .... the 2012 Olympics when he was only twenty-four years old. Jonny came third in **(7)** .... race. The brothers do so well **(8)** .... they work very hard.

VOCABULARY

1 Complete the text with the words and phrases in the box.

> body and health   family   friends
> schoolwork   sport

2 What is the most important thing in your life? Put the words and phrases in the box in Exercise 1 in order of importance for you (1 = most important).

1 ....   2 ....   3 ....
4 ....   5 ....

What is the most important thing
in your life?

Olga
At the moment it's my **(1)** .... I'm only fourteen, but I already know what I want to do when I'm older. I want to be a doctor. That means I have to work really hard.

Sergey
The most important thing for me is my
(2) .... We've all got to look after ourselves. I do yoga every day and it makes me feel great. I don't eat cake or chocolate and I make sure I get a good night's sleep.

Michael
I don't think anything is more important to me than my
(3) .... We do everything together – go to the cinema, do sports, study. I tell them things I'd never tell my parents or my brother!

Paulina
My **(4)** .... are more important to me than anything. We spend a lot of time together. We always eat our evening meal together. Sometimes there are fifteen of us around the table – that's when my cousins come to dinner!

Isabella
That's easy: **(5)** ....! I live for it. I do it six days a week. I don't do anything on Sundays because I'm always tired, then. I watch it too.

GRAMMAR   First conditional

3 Complete the sentences with the correct form of the words in brackets.

1 What will we do if it .... (rain) tomorrow?
2 I won't listen to this music if you .... (not like) it.
3 They'll be really excited if we .... (get) them tickets to the concert.
4 He can .... (borrow) my football shirt if he can't find his.
5 If Alma .... (work) hard, she'll do well in her exams.
6 If I pass my exams, I .... (be) really happy.
7 If Maria .... (not go) now, she'll miss the concert.
8 If you do some exercise, you .... (feel) better.
9 If it's hot and sunny at the weekend, we .... (go) swimming with my friends.
10 If you .... (eat) more fruit and vegetables, you'll be healthier.

4 Write sentences in the first conditional.

1 If / I finish my project / I come to / the cinema

....

....

2 We feel better / if / we exercise / five times
a week

....

....

3 She / learn Portuguese / if / she move to Brazil

....

....

4 They / miss the train / if / they not leave now

....

....

5 If / we win / the match on Saturday / we be
very happy

....

....

6 If / he work hard / he pass his Russian exam

....

....

5 ⊙ Students often make mistakes with the first conditional. Correct the mistakes in these sentences.

1 If you come too, you love it.

....

2 I think it be OK if we meet at the park at ten
o'clock in the morning.

....

....

3 I will bring some banana pancake for you if my
mom made it for me.

....

....

4 If you don't have any, I give you some.

....

5 If you can visit Vietnam, I'll took you to Vung
Tau and lots of beautiful places.

....

....

LISTENING

6 ▶18 Listen to teenagers talking to a radio presenter. Match the people to the things they worry about the most.

1	Carly	a	parents
2	Paul	b	food
3	Joni	c	schoolwork
4	Neil	d	friends
5	Kate	e	sleep

7 ▶18 Listen again. Are the sentences right (✔) or wrong (✗)?

1 Carly never stays up late using the
internet. ....

2 Paul likes getting up late. ....

3 Joni doesn't like chocolate. ....

4 Neil is fourteen years old. ....

5 Kate usually keeps her ideas to herself. ....

WRITING

8 Complete the text with the words in the box.

> feel   forget   go   if   sleep
> studying   worry   worried

I (1) .... most about exams
in school. (2) .... there's
an exam, I get very (3) ....
a few days before I have to do it. Then I
don't (4) .... very well and
I think about all the things that could go
wrong. On the day of the exam I usually
(5) .... very tired, so I worry
that I will (6) .... everything
I know. My mother gave me some good advice
the last time I was worrying about exams.
She says that I should take a break from
(7) .... and do something
different. That is what I try to do. I
(8) .... for a swim, listen to
music, and try my best not to worry too much.
But it's not easy!

9 Now write about something that worries you.

....

....

....

....

....

....

....

....

....

18 Expedition!
It may rain on Sunday

VOCABULARY

1 Choose the right words to complete the conversation.

Mum: OK. Have you got everything?

Jean: I'm not sure.

Mum: Your hands will be cold in the mountains. Have you got your **(1)** *boots / gloves*?

Jean: Yes, I've packed them.

Mum: Did you put extra pairs of **(2)** *socks / trousers* in? Your feet will be cold too.

Jean: Yes, I've packed lots of them. I've also got lots of T-shirts, hats and sunglasses.

Mum: You're only taking one pair of **(3)** *sweaters / trousers*, aren't you?

Jean: That's right, but I'm not taking my jeans. But I've packed a couple of thick **(4)** *socks / sweaters* too. I want to make sure I'm warm at night.

Mum: Good idea. Are you going to wear your **(5)** *boots / towel* all the time?

Jean: Yes, I am. I'm not taking another pair of shoes.

Mum: Have you packed a **(6)** *gloves / towel*? The ones at the expedition centre might be a bit old.

Jean: Of course I have! I've got a bar of soap too.

Mum: Great. All right. What about food and drink?

Jean: I've packed a **(7)** *bowl / water bottle* for my breakfast cereal. I've also got a plate, a spoon, a knife and a **(8)** *fork / snacks*. Oh, and a big **(9)** *fork / water bottle*. I've put that in the top of my bag.

Mum: Good idea. All that walking will make you very thirsty. What about a **(10)** *bowl / mug* for hot drinks?

Jean: Yes, I've packed one.

Mum: Oh, you'll need to buy some **(11)** *playing cards / snacks* as well.

Jean: I know. I want to get some fruit and some biscuits.

Mum: Sounds good. What about something to play?

Jean: Well, I've packed some **(12)** *mug / playing cards*.

Mum: Great. Do you know many games?

Jean: No, but Polly does. She can teach me!

GRAMMAR   *may/might*

2 Choose the right word to complete the sentences.

1 I *may / may not* go to the cinema tonight. I've got lots of homework to do.

2 Let's take lots of snacks. We *might / might not* get very hungry!

3 She *might / might not* come to the party. She's feeling very tired.

4 I *may / may not* take my umbrella. I don't want to get wet if it rains.

5 They *might / might not* be able to play tennis because the weather is so bad.

3 Write about what you may do. Complete the sentences.

1 I may .... this weekend.

2 I may .... in the summer.

3 I may .... next year.

4 I may .... after I leave school.

5 One day, I may ....

4 🔘 Students often make mistakes with *may* and *might*. Which sentence is right (✔)?

1 **a** I left my diary at your house yesterday. I think it might be in the sitting room. ....
 b I left my diary at your house yesterday. I think it can be in the sitting room. ....

2 **a** I think you should wear a raincoat because I think tomorrow we will have rain. ....
 b I think you might wear a raincoat because I think tomorrow we will have rain. ....

3 **a** In the morning we are going to visit the 'Old City' and might we going to go the cinema. ....
 b In the morning we are going to visit the 'Old City' and we might go to the cinema. ....

4 **a** I left my umbrella in your room. Bring it to me later. It might rain at any moment. ....
 b I left my umbrella in your room. Bring it to me later. It must rain at any moment. ....

5 **a** First I want to go swimming and cycling. Then we can go sightseeing! ....
 b First I want to go swimming and cycling. Then we may go sightseeing! ....

READING

GREAT ADVENTURES

EXAM TIPS

Reading Part 4 (three-text matching)
• Look to see if the writer says the same thing in a different way.
• The questions do not follow the order of information in the texts.

Lisa
I travelled around the world by boat just after my twentieth birthday. I felt sad because I didn't see my friends, but I enjoyed being on my own – it gave me time to look at the world around me. My journey was hard work. There were lots of storms. I even had to do work for university. I might write a book about what I did when I'm older.

Michael
I climbed Everest when I was nineteen. It wasn't easy! I sometimes thought 'it would be good to stop doing this', but I didn't stop. It's normal to feel tired. I often climb on my own, but I did this one with my dad. We didn't have any problems. I took a break from studying while we were climbing. I didn't miss it! You can read my book about my adventure after I have finished it!

Rod
I have travelled many times with my sister, but after I finished school, I travelled with my friend. We cycled from Portugal to Greece just before my nineteenth birthday. We stopped for a couple of days because I broke my finger, but apart from that nothing went wrong. We didn't have to do any studying because we weren't students. One day I'd like to write a book about the trip.

5 🔘 Read the articles by three young people about their adventures.
For questions 1–7, choose A, B or C.

Example:

0 Who travelled alone?	**Ⓐ** Lisa	**B** Michael	**C** Rod
1 Who wanted to finish their journey before the end?	**A** Lisa	**B** Michael	**C** Rod
2 Who had a health problem during their trip?	**A** Lisa	**B** Michael	**C** Rod
3 Who did some studying during their trip?	**A** Lisa	**B** Michael	**C** Rod
4 Who missed their friends?	**A** Lisa	**B** Michael	**C** Rod
5 Who was with a member of their family?	**A** Lisa	**B** Michael	**C** Rod
6 Who is writing a book?	**A** Lisa	**B** Michael	**C** Rod
7 Who did their journey at the youngest age?	**A** Lisa	**B** Michael	**C** Rod

It was hard to wake Dylan up

VOCABULARY Phrasal verbs

1 Complete the sentences with the verbs in the box. Use one verb twice.

> get   give   lie   pick   put
> take   try   wake   wash

1 My parents always .... me up from football practice.
2 What time did you .... back from the party?
3 My mum and dad find it very easy to .... up in the morning. The alarm clock rings, they wake up, and a few seconds later they're out of bed and in the kitchen making breakfast.
4 Could you .... off your shoes, please?
5 I'm tired, so I'm going to .... down for a while.
6 I don't .... up very easily. Without my alarm clock, I'd sleep until lunchtime!
7 My brothers never .... up. They leave their dirty cups and plates on the sofa, on the kitchen table, and in their rooms.
8 Why don't you .... on this T-shirt?
9 My friends never .... back the things I lend to them.
10 It's cold today, you should .... your scarf on.

2 Complete the sentences with the phrasal verbs from Exercise 1.

1 Brian is .... because he's got a headache.
2 I .... my cap .... because the sun was shining in my eyes.
3 Can you .... me .... my ruler when you finish using it?
4 I forgot to .... my trainers .... after football practice and got the carpet dirty.
5 I slept for a long time last night. I didn't .... until 8.30!
6 Can I .... the pair of trousers .... , please?
7 I never cook the dinner in our house, but I always .... afterwards.
8 After my alarm clock rings, I usually stay in bed for five minutes before I ....
9 I'm so tired. We didn't .... from our trip until really late last night.
10 Can you .... me .... from Liam's birthday party tomorrow evening?

LISTENING

3 ▶19 Listen to Mark and John talking about an expedition. Are the sentences right (✔) or wrong (✗)?

1 John's expedition starts on Sunday. ....
2 John has only got one brother. ....
3 John's older sister is studying at university. ....
4 John is going to Wales. ....
5 John has been to Snowdonia before. ....
6 John enjoys packing. ....
7 John never forgets to pack anything. ....
8 John will be away for five days. ....

4 ▶19 Listen again and number the sentences from the recording in the right order.

a My younger sister's coming too. ....
b My brother wants to stay an extra day. ....
c It's so boring. ....
d Oh no! ....
e I can't wait. ....
f Have you been there before? ....

Prepare to write a description of an expedition

5 Match the two halves of the sentences.

1 We walked
2 We stayed at a campsite
3 I listened to music
4 We all swam in the river,
5 It was my first trip

a without my parents. They stayed at home.
b around the town and we looked at the old buildings.
c except my brother Neil.
d between a castle and a museum. There were lots of people staying there.
e during the long journey home. My brother and sister fell asleep!

6 Complete the sentences with the words in the box.

> around   between   during   except   without

1 We looked out of the window and listened to music .... the journey to the campsite.
2 When we got to the campsite, we looked .... for a good place for our tent.
3 We camped in a beautiful place .... the trees and the river.
4 The next day I got up early and went out for a walk .... my family.
5 Everyone walked up the big mountain near the campsite, ... Curtis. He wasn't feeling very well.

7 Complete the text with the verbs in the box.

> carry   cooking   have   meet   rained   stayed   walking   went

Last spring I (1) .... on an expedition with my family to the Urals in Russia. It is one of the most beautiful places I (2) .... ever been to.

We (3) .... at a really good campsite which had showers, a games room and a kitchen. There was also a really big room where we could (4) .... the other people at the campsite. We played cards most evenings.

Every day we went (5) .... in the mountains. One day we walked 15 kilometres. I was very tired that evening!

I didn't like the weather very much. It (6) .... a lot, and it was cold and windy. But I was very glad to learn how to read a map and I enjoyed (7) .... sausages for everyone. My parents also taught me how to put up and take down a tent.

We stayed at the campsite for six days and we walked every day. We had to (8) .... our heavy backpacks full of snacks, drinks and clothes. It was hard work sometimes, but I can't wait to do it again!

8 Now write about an expedition you have been on.
Answer these questions:

1 Where did you go?
2 Who did you go with?
3 Where did you stay?
4 What did you do?
5 What did you like and dislike?
6 How long did you stay?

....
....
....
....
....
....
....
....

19 Different ingredients
They are eaten with milk

VOCABULARY

1 Find eight verbs used to talk about cooking.

p	r	e	p	a	r	e
h	t	s	f	d	q	c
a	c	m	k	d	r	y
n	b	o	i	l	p	j
u	g	e	v	x	d	o
l	b	a	k	e	i	r
f	i	l	l	m	r	b

2 Complete the sentences with the correct form of the verbs from Exercise 1.

1 You can .... fruit in the sun.
2 Could you .... some water? I'd really like a cup of tea.
3 .... the bowl with a plate and then put it in the fridge.
4 My brother has .... my mother a cake for her birthday.
5 You need to .... it all together in large bowl.
6 Have you .... any salt or pepper to this?
7 I've .... lunch. Are you ready to eat?
8 Would you .... the bowl with water, please?

GRAMMAR   Present simple passive

3 Match the two halves of the sentences.

1 Tea is drunk   ....
2 Italian wine is   ....
3 Beans are grown in   ....
4 Lots of chocolate   ....
5 Soup is often   ....

a is produced in Belgium.
b eaten cold in Spain.
c without milk in my country.
d sold all over the world.
e Mexico.

4 Put the words in the right order to make sentences.

1 grown / countries / many / tomatoes / are / in
....
....

2 made / fruit / from / is / jam
....

3 sold / airports / at / books / are
....

4 produced / coffee / Brazil / is / in
....

5 Switzerland / four languages / in / spoken / are
....
....

5 ⊚ Students often make mistakes with the present simple passive. Correct the mistakes in four of these sentences. Which two sentences are correct?

1 The art lesson is started at ten o'clock.
....
....

2 You start off from your house, turn left, go straight on, take the second right, and you are arrived there.
....
....
....

3 Coffee is drunk all over the world.
....
....

4 You can get the number 12 bus. It is stopped near my house.
....
....

5 The class lasts two hours and we are spent the time painting.
....
....

READING

6 **Number the paragraphs in the right order.**

Life in my kitchen

ⓐ ☐ So that's life in my kitchen. My family really loves being there. We listen to music, talk and laugh. It's my favourite place at home. But don't talk about the washing up!

ⓑ ☐ Breakfast is a busy time for everyone. Mum and Dad have to go to work and my brother and I have to go to school. But we take time to sit down at the kitchen table to eat together. We usually have cereal, toast, tea, coffee and orange juice. Mum has fruit sometimes, but Dad always has toast. He has the same thing every day!

ⓒ ☐ We only have lunch together at the weekend and in the holidays. We often have fish, fresh bread and salad. My brother makes really nice salads. Lunch is usually a meal that we prepare quite quickly.

ⓓ ☐ Today I want to write about my kitchen – it's the centre of our home. Everyone in my family loves cooking, so we spend a lot of time in the kitchen. We don't worry if things fall on the floor and get untidy when we are cooking. The time to tidy up is after breakfast, lunch and dinner – not before!

ⓔ ☐ We have lots of different things for dinner. My sister makes fantastic pizza – I love it! My mother loves it too! It's really good! We often have fruit afterwards, but sometimes we have chocolate cake. I sometimes make it. My dad can make chocolate cake too. His is much better than mine. Dinner is my favourite meal of the day. Everyone is home from work and school, and we sit at the kitchen table eating and talking for a long time.

7 **Read the text again and match the people to the information.**

1 Mum   **a** makes the best chocolate cake
2 Dad   **b** makes pizza
3 Brother   **c** sometimes has fruit for breakfast
4 Sister   **d** is good at making salad

WRITING

8 **Write a description of your family's meal times. Answer these questions:**

1 What do you usually have for breakfast, lunch and dinner?
2 Where do you eat? (e.g. kitchen, dining room)
3 Who prepares the meals?
4 Do you and your family have a favourite meal?
5 Who washes up the dirty dishes?

....
....
....
....
....
....

I hope you like my blog

VOCABULARY

1 Look at the pictures and write the words.

> beans   carrots   garlic   melon   pear
> potatoes   salt and pepper   steak

1 ....

2 ....

3 ....

4 ....

5 ....

6 ....

7 ....

8 ....

2 Complete the sentences with adjectives.

1 Would you like a f _ _ _ _ egg?
2 We had g _ _ _ _ _ _ fish last night.
3 I really like b _ _ _ _ _ rice.
4 We're having b _ _ _ _ potatoes and sausages for dinner.
5 Let's have r _ _ _ _ chicken on Sunday.

3 Complete the table with the words in the box.

> bowl   cup   dish   fork   glass   knife   mug   plate   spoon

eat with	drink from	put food in or on
....	....	....
....	....	....
....	....	....

4 Choose the right verb to complete the phrases.

1 *make / do* a cake
2 *make / do* the cleaning
3 *make / do* a cup of tea
4 *make / do* the dishes
5 *make / do* your homework
6 *make / do* a mess
7 *make / do* a mistake
8 *make / do* the shopping
9 *make / do* the washing
10 *make / do* the bed

5 Complete the sentences with the correct form of *make* or *do*.

1 The washing machine broke when I was .... the washing yesterday.
2 When I visit my grandmother, the first thing she says to me is 'Would you like me to .... you a cup of tea?'
3 My baby brother .... a mess when he eats.
4 My parents always .... the cleaning at the weekend.
5 My sister .... me a beautiful cake for my birthday last week.
6 Have you .... your bed?
7 My friends think I'm crazy, but I enjoy .... my homework.
8 Do you ever .... the dishes at home?
9 I've .... the shopping lots of times, but I don't enjoy it.
10 I usually .... a lot of mistakes when I speak another language.

6 What do you do at home? What don't you do? Write sentences with *make* and *do* phrases from Exercise 4 and the words in the box.

> always   usually   often   sometimes   never

1 ....
2 ....
3 ....
4 ....

LISTENING

EXAM TIPS

Listening Part 4

• Don't decide that something is the right answer just because you have heard it. Listen carefully.
• Look at the notes before you listen and think about the kind of information you need to write.

7 ● ▶20 **You will hear Jason talking to Nora about his birthday meal. Listen and complete each question. You will hear the conversation twice.**

JASON'S BIRTHDAY MEAL

Name of restaurant: ....Roberto's........

Day: **(1)** ....

Time: **(2)** .... pm

Cost of meal: **(3)** £................................. per person.

Address of restaurant: **(4)** 74 .... Street.

Restaurant is opposite: **(5)** ....

VOCABULARY

1 Put the letters in the right order to make words for places in a town.

1 otlhe ....
2 tahedrcla ....
3 maksepuertr ....
4 afcoyrt ....
5 ecalst ....
6 suomeq ....
7 rlairyb ....
8 psorst etncer ....
....
9 istnaot ....
10 etahret ....

2 Complete the sentences with words from Exercise 1.

1 I like to stay in a .... when we go on holiday, but my brother prefers going camping.
2 My parents go to the .... twice a month. They enjoy watching old plays.
3 The .... in our town is great. I usually go swimming and play badminton there.
4 I don't like going to the .... I much prefer smaller shops.
5 Our train arrived late at the ....
6 My dad thinks that the .... in our town will close because everyone is reading eBooks.

GRAMMAR   Past simple passive

3 Complete the sentences with the correct form of the verbs.

1 The Statue of Liberty .... (give) to the USA by France.
2 A film .... (make) in our library. My brother and I were in it!
3 The cathedral and castle in our town .... (visit) by thousands of tourists last summer.
4 The new museum .... (complete) in 2012.
5 The old church near my house .... (turn into) a hotel a few years ago.
6 Our sports centre and theatre .... (close) a long time ago.
7 Buckingham Palace .... (build) in the 18th century.

4 👁 Students often make mistakes with the past simple passive. Correct the mistakes in these sentences.

1 My old shorts was eaten by my dog.
....
2 I am selling my little home in the centre of town. It was build 25 years ago.
....
....
3 My birthday party was very enjoyable. All the people were danced.
....
....
4 My mobile is fantastic. It were made in Mexico.
....
5 Do you know about my new flat? I was moved two weeks ago.
....
....

IRONBRIDGE

a prize-winning area of museums

EXAM TIPS

Reading Part 4 (right, wrong, or doesn't say)
- Look for and highlight the parts of the texts where you think the answers can be found.
- Only choose C if you can't find the information in the text.

In the late 18th century, a man called Abraham Darby III built the world's first iron bridge, across the River Severn in England. He also built houses for his factory workers to live in and he was popular because he paid them more money than other factories did.

Today, the whole area of Ironbridge is a group of ten living museums, where visitors can learn about history and see how things like iron and glass were made 100 years ago. To make Ironbridge seem real, most of its staff dress in 19th-century clothes. Visitors can dress like this for a special photo at the old photographer's shop, at any time of the day they choose.

Tourists like to visit the bridge and the old factories, as well as the different houses where people lived. The tables and chairs inside Rosehill House and Dale House were actually used by members of the Darby family, and people usually spend at least an hour looking at everything there. It takes even longer to walk around Blists Hill, which is a complete Victorian town, with an old bank, a sweet shop, a chemist's and several other shops.

5 ● **Read the article about Ironbridge, where you can learn about life 100 years ago. Are the sentences 'Right' (A) or 'Wrong' (B)? If there is not enough information to answer 'Right' (A) or 'Wrong' (B), choose 'Doesn't say' (C).**

Example:

0 Abraham Darby III's bridge was built in the second half of the 18th century.

(A) Right   B Wrong   C Doesn't say

1 Darby's workers earned less than in other factories.

A Right   B Wrong   C Doesn't say

2 The ten museums at Ironbridge have different opening times.

A Right   B Wrong   C Doesn't say

3 It is possible to watch someone making glass in an old way.

A Right   B Wrong   C Doesn't say

4 Some of the people working at Ironbridge wear modern clothes.

A Right   B Wrong   C Doesn't say

5 Visitors have to book an appointment at the old photographer's shop.

A Right   B Wrong   C Doesn't say

6 The rooms in Dale House still have furniture belonging to the Darby family.

A Right   B Wrong   C Doesn't say

7 Visitors usually spend more time in the two Darby homes than in Blist Hill.

A Right   B Wrong   C Doesn't say

A big change in my life

VOCABULARY

1 Look at the pictures and write the words.

> detective   farmer   police officer   radio presenter
> receptionist   taxi driver   waitress

1 ....

2 ....

3 ....

4 ....

5 ....

6 ....

7 ....

2 Complete the text with jobs from Exercise 1.

My sister has done lots of jobs. She was a (1) ....
for a year, but she didn't enjoy driving. Then she was a
(2) .... in a hotel, but she didn't like giving the guests
the keys to their rooms. She was a (3) .... in a French
restaurant for six months. But that job made her hungry all the time.

Then she got a job as a (4) .... 'You're so lucky,' I
said. 'You've got your own programme on the radio!' Jess didn't think
she was lucky. She presented the Breakfast Show, so she had to get
up at three o'clock in the morning.

She's a (5) .... now. She's not enjoying it very much. 'It's
like being a taxi driver,' she says. 'I spend most of the day in the
car.' She's thinking of becoming a (6) .... at the moment.
She wants to be like Sherlock Holmes.

3 Read the sentences. Is *change* a noun (N) or a verb (V)?

0 Does Arlo want to change his job? .....V....

1 Please let us know your change of address. ....

2 Can you change a twenty-pound note? ....

3 It was a long journey. We had to change trains four times. ....

4 Can I change this video game, please? ....

5 Bring a change of clothes for the trip. It's going to snow! ....

4 Complete the sentences with the correct form of the verb *change*.

1 OK. Let's look at our journey – we're .... planes in Bangkok and then we're flying on to Sydney.

2 I had the receipt, so it was easy to .... my shoes for a bigger pair.

3 Going away to university when he was eighteen .... David's life.

4 Tom .... the name of his website every week!

LISTENING

5 ▶21 **Listen to the conversation between Patty and Robert and choose the right answer (a or b).**

1 Robert is moving to ....
a York **b** Liverpool

2 Robert says the bus is .... than the train.
a cheaper **b** more expensive

3 Robert's .... has got a new job.
a father **b** mother

4 Robert's mother is going to .... at the university.
a work **b** study

5 Robert .... excited to be moving.
a is **b** isn't

6 Robert's new school is ....
a small **b** big

Prepare to write a biography

6 **Number the paragraphs in the right order.**

a ☐ When he finished school, he went to Exeter University to study history. He did well at university. After he finished studying, he got a job at Durham University. He really enjoyed his job. He liked teaching students. He also liked reading and writing books about the history of 20th century Britain. But he didn't play the piano any more.

b ☐ My father was born in Edinburgh, Scotland, on the 5th of January, 1970. When he was a boy, his parents bought him a piano. He started playing it every day and became very good at it.

c ☐ One day, before I was born, he went with my mother to watch someone play the piano. When he was watching the concert, he remembered how much he liked the piano. That night he decided to change his life. He began playing the piano again and six months later he started his own band. People couldn't believe it when he left his good job at the university, but Dad has worked as a piano player for twenty years now and it still makes him very happy. He says 'you have to do what you love.'

7 **Choose the best title for the text in Exercise 6.**

a A biography of my father ....
b Dad's university life ....
c The story of the piano ....

8 **Write a short biography of an adult you know. Include this information:**

1 where and when the person was born
2 what they loved doing as a child
3 the job they do as an adult
4 a change the person has made in their life

....
....
....
....
....
....
....
....
....

Acknowledgements

Development of this publication has made use of the Cambridge English Corpus, a multi-billion word collection of spoken and written English. It includes the Cambridge Learner Corpus, a unique collection of candidate exam answers. Cambridge University Press has built up the Cambridge English Corpus to provide evidence about language use that helps to produce better language teaching materials.

This product is informed by English Profile, a Council of Europe-endorsed research programme that is providing detailed information about the language that learners of English know and use at each level of the Common European Framework of Reference (CEFR). For more information, please visit www.englishprofile.org

The authors and publishers acknowledge the following sources of copyright material and are grateful for the permissions granted. While every effort has been made, it has not always been possible to identify the sources of all the material used, or to trace all copyright holders. If any omissions are brought to our notice, we will be happy to include the appropriate acknowledgements on reprinting.

Photo acknowledgements

p. 8: (T/L) Wolf Avni/Shutterstock, (T/C) Rafael Martin-Gaitero/Shutterstock, (T/R) Gratien Jonxis/Shutterstock, (B/L) Nemar74/Shutterstock, (B/C) George Rodger/Getty, (B/R) Pal Teravagimov/Shutterstock; p: 11 (T) Four Oaks/Shutterstock, (B) Airn/Shutterstock; p. 13 GeoPic/Alamy; p: 15 (T) Tagstock1/Shutterstock, (CT) Emilio Gomez/Shutterstock, (CB) Hamideddine Bouali/Corbis, (B) Religious Images/UIG/Getty; p. 19: (T) Martin Child/Getty, (C) jennyt/Shutterstock, (B) StfW/Alamy; p.26: Florilegius/Alamy; p. 30: Roussel Bernard/Alamy; p. 31: Pyty/Shutterstock; p. 38: ZUMA Press, Inc./Alamy; p. 39: Ivan Arlandis/ActionPlusCorbis; p. 41: Inti St Clair/Getty; p. 43: (T) Wikimedia unified mark is a trademark of the Wikimedia Foundation and is used with the permission of the Wikimedia Foundation. They are not endorsed by or affiliated with the Wikimedia Foundation. (B) Syda Productions/Shutterstock; p. 44: (TL) JM Travel Photography/Shutterstock, (TC) ivavrb/Shutterstock, (TR) Ramon Espelt Photography/Shutterstock, (CL) lillisphotography/Getty, (C) Ramon Espelt Photography/Shutterstock, (CR) Brian Kinney/Shutterstock, (BL) Celso Diniz/Shutterstock, (BC) Joakim Lloyd Raboff/Shutterstock; p. 45: Tim Dobbs/Shutterstock; p. 61: Oliver Strewe/Getty; p. 67: Janine Wiedel Photolibrary/Alamy; p. 69: epa european pressphoto agency b.v./Alamy; p.73: (T) Halfpoint/Shutterstock, (C) Lithiumphoto/Shutterstock, (B) l i g h t p o e t/Shutterstock; p. 75: Alexander Ishchenko/Shutterstock; p. 77: Golden Pixels LLC/Shutterstock; p. 80: Renata Sedmakova/Shutterstock; p. 81: Robin Weaver/Alamy.

Front cover photo by Monkey Business Images/Shutterstock.

Illustrations

Ilias Arahovitis (Beehive Illustration) pp. 28 (T), 54; Russ Cook pp. 14, 21 (R), 28 (B), 55, 58, 71, 82; Nigel Dobbyn (Beehive Illustration) pp. 6, 8, 12, 16, 33, 47, 56, 65; Mark Draisey pp. 4, 10,13, 24, 53, 57, 63, 72; Mark Duffin pp. 27, 32, 40, 48, 66, 78; Tony Forbes (Sylvie Poggio Artists Agency) pp. 21 (L), 22, 25, 35, 51, 62, 70; Pablo Velarde pp. 36, 60, 83.

The publishers are grateful to the following contributors:
text design and layouts: emc design Ltd; cover design: Andrew Ward; picture research: emc design Ltd; audio recordings: produced by IH Sound and recorded at DSound, London; edited by Liz Driscoll.